THE LITTLE WAY

THE LITTLE WAY

The Spirituality of Thérèse of Lisieux

BERNARD BRO o.p.

Translated by ALAN NEAME

Darton, Longman & Todd
London

First published in English in 1979
Darton, Longman & Todd Ltd
89 Lillie Road, London SW6 1UD

Translation © Darton, Longman & Todd Ltd, 1979

Originally published as *La Gloire et le Mendiant*
by Les Editions du Cerf, 29 boulevard Latour-Maubourg, Paris VII[e]

© Les Editions du Cerf, 1974

ISBN 0 232 51420 8

Printed in Great Britain by the Anchor Press Ltd
and bound by Wm Brendon & Son Ltd,
both of Tiptree, Essex

THE BEGGAR

Once he was hidden from us, now he has become us
Once he was one of us, now he has become us.

He, the King, has come down, Lord of the supreme throne,
A beggar, although none other can be king.

The master of the house has become the house itself,
The taker of hearts has submitted to How and to Why.

Neither riches nor poverty hold him in obedience,
He has put on the poor man's smock to show us what wealth is.

The flawless gem, the inestimable jewel,
Has germinated to be the earth and heavens.

MAGHRIBI
(Fourteenth-century Persian mystic)

CONTENTS

PREFACE

A growing child, aware that grown-ups have explanations for everything, asks why God made the world. And here, as it happens, a
child can give us the answer. We only have to listen to what she has
to say. As usual, there are plenty of reasons for not doing so. But
since the earliest days of Christianity, no one has ever provided a
more direct or inspired short-cut to the Gospel.

In the vineyards of the part of the world where I come from, there
are two critical moments in the year: the frosts in late April and early
May, and the amount of sunshine at the end of September. The
margin is minute: two degrees below zero and the buds can survive,
four degrees or more and all is lost. Even if the summer is a wash-
out, a few days of sunshine before the grape-harvest—if you are
patient enough to wait—will save the situation.

So it is with our lives as Christians. The margin is minute. Youthful or adult years may be mis-spent or a wash-out. But the situation
can still be saved. Provided you wish it so. To my mind, the life and
example of Thérèse of Lisieux are those few days of unexpected
sunshine before harvest. The little way is practically nothing at all,
and yet it can save the situation.

If you know all about her life already, you can begin at Chapter 3.
The book is constructed of pairs of chapters on charity, Chapters
3—4; hope, Chapters 5—6; mercy, Chapters 7—8; knowledge of
God and the achievement of happiness, Chapters 9—10.

This book is not intended to be a study *of* the life of Thérèse of
Lisieux but *an introduction to life with* Thérèse of Lisieux.

BIBLIOGRAPHICAL NOTE

Quotations throughout the book are the translator's own version; in many cases no English translation exists. The main texts are Thérèse's *L'Histoire d'une Ame*, *Correspondance générale*, *Derniers Entretiens*, and *Poésies*. Others cited include *Conseils et souvenirs*, edited by Sister Geneviève, the official accounts of the Procès or canonization proceedings, and *Fondation III: Fondation du Carmel de Lisieux*, III (1857–1904).

Available in English are *Autobiography of a Saint: The Story of a Soul* (Collins Fontana) and Thérèse's *Collected Letters*, tr. F. J. Sheed (Sheed & Ward).

1

A PRACTICAL JOKE

'You are to love the Lord with all your strength, and your neighbour as much as yourself.' This is the programme. And that anyone should have carried the programme out by such simple means has justifiably been hailed as one of the Holy Spirit's 'practical jokes'. In a word, God's most exalted secrets for the world today, hidden under the most commonplace of externals. The same thing applies in the lives of all the saints and even in the life of Christ at Nazareth. We think we know it all, then find that we haven't yet discovered anything: far from being the sweet little Norman girl, the Carmelite assigned to hug an armful of roses, she was a warrior. And yet this is what Fr Karl Rahner, one of the greatest luminaries of Catholic thought for the past thirty years has to say about her in *Christliche Innerlichkeit*: 'I find many aspects of this saint's personality and writings irritating or merely boring. And if I were to explain what I find almost repulsive about them so that you could see why, it certainly wouldn't justify the trouble of doing so. There are so many other things worth thinking about in the world and not needing elaborate explanation.' There you have it in a nutshell: 'irritating', 'boring' and 'repulsive'. . . .

Fr Rahner wasn't the first in the field. Shortly before St Thérèse's death, one of her fellow-nuns remarked: 'Our Sister Thérèse of the Child Jesus will soon be dead, and I really can't imagine what Reverend Mother will find to say about her once she is gone. It won't be easy for her, I can tell you; for this little sister, charming as she is, has certainly never done anything worth the telling.' True. So how are we to place Thérèse of Lisieux? There are so many apparent obstacles: the cultural gap, 'the benighted nineteeth century'; the gap in life-style: a provincial middle-class girl who takes the veil; the spirituality gap: the cult of suffering, of asceticism, of the Rule; ignorance of collective and political life; the antithesis between the world, 'this vale of tears', and heaven as the only centre of interest, etc. Appearances are certainly discouraging. Possibly she did have, at one particular moment, some useful contribution to make to the Church? But why should we waste our time over that now?

I have spent a long time examining these objections and my conclusion is that they don't hold water, they make a caricature of her life and thought. These objections invariably stem from ignorance and are the result of our inevitable tendency to degrade whatever is great. The mechanism is a subtle one. First we create an idea in our own minds, so that we don't have to go and look for ourselves. Then, we take things a step further. And we end up by saying, as Thérèse herself would also have said, 'What does Thérèse matter anyway?' So much for the clearest and simplest abridgement of the Gospel ever propounded.

One of the best approaches to the way we should look at Thérèse of Lisieux is offered by one of those Christian master-minds who was also active in politics: Emmanuel Mounier. You would hardly expect to get the key to her works from someone like him, but in 1939 he wrote: 'One of the chief obstacles we have found has always been the middle-class style in which the saint disguised her heroism. At each point, nonetheless, her life offers us the key to absolute detachment. And in an age when the middle-class point of view cannot fail to seem the very antithesis of Christian living, mayn't it be that this is one of the Holy Spirit's practical jokes—a paradox of Divine Mercy—I mean, that the mysteries of love at its most ardent should be deliberately hidden under such commonplace externals?'

'One of the Holy Spirit's practical jokes. . . .'

When I observe how little known she still is among my closest contemporaries, my family, my friends, and how rarely they seem even to have read what she wrote, when it takes so little time to do so, 'Yes,' I think, 'this is certainly one of the Holy Spirit's jokes.' And the best thing one can do in the circumstances is to make people want to read or re-read her. You don't really know her, you see. I calculate that to read the essential parts of what she said and wrote would take half as long as a Russian novel. So let's now open this volume of stories and pictures, in which we see death and despair at war with youth and afflicted innocence, the struggle between darkness and faith, between the real and the counterfeit, between maturity and childhood. It is one of the liveliest books imaginable. Providentially available. Contemporary. You may think you know all about it already, as I thought I did. But in fact there is no end to rediscovering its freshness, its acuteness, its immediacy, its strength, its genius indeed 'under the most commonplace externals'. But beware: the book doesn't evade the issues. It deals with the most serious and least escapable questions of life: why death? how are we to hope to the last? can we experience religious doubts, be shaken by them and still stay faithful? why do we have to suffer? Possibly one ought to have loved or suffered already before one can understand the book properly, just as one has to have loved and suffered before one can understand the Gospels.

A statue to be stripped?

In 1949 when Stalinism was at its height, the afore-mentioned Emmanuel Mounier in public correspondence with one of France's leading Communist intellectuals wondered what he could wish the latter for good. This is what he wrote: 'We would not particularly have wished you Tito; what we do wish you are the individual or collective equivalents of a St Thérèse.'

Three months before the 1914 war, Pope Pius X, wishing to offer Christians a model for their lives, said of Thérèse that she was 'the greatest saint of modern times'. She was beatified nine years later when, had she lived, she would have been fifty. She was canonised another two years later in 1925. Since then, that middle-class girl who entered Carmel at the age of fifteen to seek oblivion and self-effacement there, exclusively preoccupied with loving Jesus, and dying of tuberculosis at the age of twenty-four like many other girls in the nineteenth century—this nobody the centenary of whose birth was celebrated in 1973—has subsequently affected the lives of millions: from Edith Piaf to the last five popes.

The life of Thérèse of Lisieux has run through eighty-nine editions, has been translated into thirty-five languages, including Russian, Chinese, Arabic, Turkish and Swahili. Next to the Bible, it is the most widely read religious book in French. And from Los Angeles to Ghardaia, from Beirut to Oslo, from Winnipeg to Mexico, you will find her in her Carmelite habit with her roses at the ready: undoubtedly one of the most widely revered women of the twentieth century. This being so, is it our job today to refurbish that statue, to regild that picture or consider whether Thérèse of Lisieux is only a trap for the feeble and a tranquilliser for the devout? Do we need to hear any more about her 'raining down roses'? What can a cloistered nun possibly have to say that is relevant to our struggle for a better world, she apparently having fled the world? It has been said of her that, unknown during her lifetime, she has been mis-understood ever since. But if you have to strip off the paint before you can understand her, is it really worth the effort?

But is it so sure that the paint does have to be stripped off? And Lisieux, with Windsor Castle and the Eiffel Tower, being one of the most visited places in Europe, we can hardly be the first people to have guessed the scope of the revolution which she inspired. No, indeed: popes and people understood her much sooner than intellec-tuals have.

What is she like, then?

'Mystical, comical: everything by turns'

'Tall and strong with a childlike air, with voice and expression to match, concealing the wisdom, perfection and perspicacity of a per-son of fifty . . . A little goody-goody to whom you would give com-munion without sending her to confession, but as artful as a waggon-load of monkeys. Mystical, comical: everything by turns. She can make you weep with devotion and just as easily make you faint with laughter during recreation.' This is the most vivid portrait preserved of her, penned by her Sub-Prioress when Thérèse was twenty. But is this sufficient to make her 'the greatest saint of modern times'?

Luckily we have a great deal of testimony about her. Besides her own autobiography, written at the age of twenty-two and completed three months before her death, her sisters and companions in relig-ion have left us a series of interviews, in some cases noted down from day to day, retaining the gripping fascination of a live television programme. And through the (apparent) commonplaceness of these pious videotapes, the same fact consistently emerges (today as novel as it ever was): *that with Thérèse of Lisieux, we are in the presence of someone who, faced with the two abysses which all men experience, i.e. self and God, went all the way; yet still remains our comrade.* Thérèse is pre-eminently the human being confronted with the abyss of freedom and of possibilities of choice; and confronted by an answering abyss which is called God.

All this took place at the dawn of the third major crisis of our civilisation: no longer man merely confronting his weakness (as with the Greeks); no longer man merely confronting his guilt (with Luther in Europe's tragic hour after the Black Death in the late Middle Ages); but modern man confronting his loneliness and the desperate quest for a meaning to life—man, every individual, haunted by the quest for a postulated 'authentic existence', that 'true life' seemingly never quite within reach. Of the countless witnesses whom we might cross-examine on this topic, I cite only two as seeming best to express that ultimate questioning, shared too by Thérèse:

'There's my old pain again, down in the pit of my stomach, like an ulcer, hurting whenever I move. I know what it's called. Its name is fear of being alone for ever. And to this, I fear, there is no answer' (Camus).

'I prayed, I pleaded for a sign, I sent Heaven messages: no reply. Heaven doesn't even know my name. I kept wondering what I was in God's eyes. Now I know the answer: nothing. God doesn't see me, God doesn't hear me, God doesn't know me. You see the void above our heads? That is God. You see this hole in the ground? That's what God is. You see this crack in the door? That's God too. Silence is God. Absence is God. God is human loneliness' (Sartre).

And Thérèse too experienced this *angst:*

'When, exhausted by the darkness surrounding me, I try to refresh my heart with the memory of the luminous country to which I aspire, my torment grows twice as great. Borrowing sinners' voices, the darkness seems to mock me, saying: "You dream of light, of a homeland redolent with sweetest perfumes, you dream of eternally possessing the Creator of all these marvels, you believe that one day you'll emerge from the surrounding fog! Keep going! Keep going! Look forward to death but it will not give you what you hope for—only deeper darkness than ever, the darkness of extinction." '

For years, Thérèse tried to find what her role in society was. True, she had become a nun, but she still did not feel that she had got to the bottom of the problem. One day, she got it. Then she wrote: 'To be a martyr was the dream of my youth. And in the cloisters of Carmel the dream grew with me. But even then I realised that my dream was absurd, because I couldn't limit my desires to a specific kind of martyrdom . . . I opened St Paul's epistles in the hopes of finding an answer. My eye chanced to fall on the 12th and 13th chapters of the First Epistle to the Corinthians. There I first read that not all can be apostles, prophets, doctors, etc . . . This answer did not satisfy my desires . . . I read on . . . and the Apostle explains how all the most perfect gifts are nothing without Love . . . At last I had found peace . . . I realised that Love covered every type of vocation, that Love was everything, that it embraced all times and places ... Then, in the excess of my delirious joy, I exclaimed: Love is my vocation!'

A struggler, a soldier

And that Thérèse was to prove throughout her life, this being a struggle against despair, and the triumph of love, all at once. When she was only four years old, her mother died. When she was nine, the sister who had taken her mother's place left her to enter Carmel. And three months after she had entered the convent herself, her dearly-loved father fell ill. He was certified and spent three years of atrocious suffering. People gossiped about it in the town and inside the convent: 'Isn't he ill because his daughters have all become nuns?' Each time, despair was near, but love summoned Thérèse to believe that all was possible. Faced with the abyss of her freedom and faced with the abyss of an invisible opposite number, God, she 'chose all', just as she had at the age of four. Thérèse was a fighter, a struggler: this didn't stop her being afraid of a spider ... and of having to battle unsuccessfully against her adolescent fears, her sensitiveness and her tormenting scruples. She admitted as much: 'Being the youngest, I wasn't used to doing things for myself ... My extreme sensitiveness made me unbearable. . . . I would weep like a Magdalen and then weep over having wept. But that lustrous night, it was 25th December, 1886, I received the grace of emerging from childhood, in a word the grace of my complete conversion. We were on our way home from midnight mass.' And Thérèse then relates how, looking foward to finding her stocking full of presents, she overheard her father say, 'Luckily, this will be the last year!' Then, instead of bursting into tears as was her wont, Thérèse consented to becoming completely changed: 'In a flash the task defeating me for ten years was achieved by Jesus, merely on the strength of my good will. In a word, I felt charity enter my heart, the need to forget myself in order to make others happy, and from that moment I have been happy myself!'

She became a soldier and remained one till she died. But she had to fight from the outset, even to enter Carmel. She was barely fifteen. She was refused. She managed to convince her father. But her uncle, then the superior of the convent and finally the bishop all refused. All right, she would go to the Pope. And the provincial chit decided to take advantage of a journey to Rome then under discussion to raise the matter with Leo XIII.

She had chosen Whitsunday 1887 to gain her father's permission: 'Everything round us was exactly to our taste, we were allowed all the freedom we could wish, and I used to say that our life was the very ideal of earthly happiness . . . To turn one's back on this had to be a free act of choice . . . I chose Whitsunday. All day I pleaded with the Holy Apostles to pray for me and to inspire me with the words which I should have to say . . . Wasn't it their job to help the timid child whom God destined by prayer and sacrifice to become the apostle of apostles?'

Her father was persuaded. But there were still the others . . . And the journey to Rome did not in fact carry the day. This is how she described her interview with the Pope: 'God subjected me to a great many ordeals before allowing me to enter Carmel. Let me tell you what happened when I visited the Pope . . . I didn't want to come home without speaking to the Pope. I said what you told me to say in your letter . . . (The poor Pope is so old that he might almost be dead. He can hardly speak at all . . .) I should like to have been able to explain my problem, but there was no way of doing so. The Holy Father simply said to me: If it is God's will, you will enter.' She had to wait. But eventually everyone had to give in to the girl who was later to say, 'I'm not afraid of anyone. I've always gone wherever I wanted. If necessary I'd have wriggled through their legs'.

One of the Holy Spirit's practical jokes. Yes, our first conclusion must inevitably be that Thérèse of Lisieux, however much she appears to be a nicely brought up little Norman miss, was a soldier, a warrior—the equal of any of the giants whom God has raised up for us, though under the most commonplace of externals: just so that we should get the point.

2

'A GREAT MAN'

In the course of a private audience with the Bishop of Bayeux and
Lisieux in 1932, Pius XI deplored the tendency to sentimentalise
Thérèse's image and then used this expression to describe her: 'A
great man.' The bishop passed the Pope's words back to her convent, where they came as something of a shock to the nuns, who were
still thinking of her as' their little angel'. But Thérèse had described
herself in similar terms as 'armed for war', echoing Teresa of Avila's
exhortation to her daughters to be 'the equal of strong men'.

There is no question of re-gilding Thérèse of Lisieux's glory. She
doesn't need that. What needs to be done is for us to disregard
pre-conceived ideas and irritating mannerisms and to realise in what
respects she is the equal of the greatest, of the giants of our history,
and for us perhaps the swiftest of guides to the Gospel.

She had indeed caused a revolution. We are only at the beginning
of it. A revolution with infinite consequences, since it is based on the
Gospel itself.

When she went into the convent, she was fifteen and a half. Inside,
life was far from being 'heaven'. And she admits: 'Nothing when I
am with Jesus—aridity, sleep! But at least there is silence! It's
strange how large my heart seems to be when I consider all the
treasures of the world, since I can see that all of them put together
could never satisfy it; yet when I consider Jesus, how small it seems
to be! I want to love him so much! To love him more than he has
ever been loved!' Inside the convent was loneliness, a penitential life,
one meal a day for seven months out of twelve; little, too little sleep;
the cold, one room only being heated; learning to live with companions not of her own choice; daily pin-pricks. Smilingly she noted:
'The refectory, where I worked as soon as I had taken the habit,
afforded me more than one occasion for putting my self-esteem in its
place, *viz*. underfoot.'

'Armed for war'

Like a warrior however, she does her best not to get wounded: 'My nature is such that fear makes me fall back; with love, I not only advance but I fly.' 'I know this from experience: when I feel nothing, when I am unable to pray or practise virtue, that is the time to look for little opportunities, for trifling ways of giving pleasure, more pleasure to Jesus than the empire of the world or even martyrdom nobly undergone. A smile, for instance, or a kindly word, when I would rather say nothing or look cross.' For the secret of her warfare, consider Nehru's remark: 'I have three enemies: the Chinese, famine and myself. But of the three the worst is me.' She very quickly came to realise that she was not going to achieve anything on the way of true life without having to fight either others, herself or illusion. Though she was to retain her childish fears to the end, she was never afraid of the truth, never afraid of 'living the truth', to quote St John: whether this applied to herself, her faults, her own limitations, her family, her community, her sisters or, in the end, death itself. She was not afraid that the truth might diminish her. Quite the reverse. Truth for her was never hurtful. For she had discovered the true way to victory: by disarming. Instead of evading the issues, of cheating, of trying to justify herself, of pulling the wool over her own eyes, as we all do to excuse our shortcomings, she would disarm, and disarm forthwith, immediately truth was involved. And thus she found something greater still: trust opening for her the gate of freedom. Certainly she was a revolutionary, not however by rebelling against other people, but by trust, immediate and absolute, to the last.

Her sister Céline, who was older than she was and entered the convent six years after her, reported that one day, watching Thérèse's behaviour, she felt momentarily discouraged and said to her, 'Oh, when I think how much I still have to acquire!' Thérèse immediately replied, 'Why don't you say: how much I have to lose!' And what she said, Thérèse herself put to the proof. I am thinking particularly of that most impressive but often least known period of her life: the last eighteen months, her last battle. There in the darkness, face to face with God and face to face with disease and death. On 2 April 1896, she spat blood for the first time, having retired to her cell, gone to bed and put out the light. Out of obédience, she did not re-light the lamp but waited till the following morning before discovering that she had indeed had a haemorrhage: 'On Good Friday, Jesus was pleased to give me the hope of soon going to see him in heaven. . I felt what seemed like a wave rising, rising and

seething to my lips. I didn't know what it was, but I thought that
perhaps I was going to die, and my soul was flooded with joy.' But
the shock was such that a few days later she entered the 'night' of
faith. Thenceforth the truths of religion were to be of no more consolation to her for the remaining eighteen months she had to live.

During her years as a Carmelite, she rediscovered the true face of
the Christian God. And did this quite on her own, like an explorer.
Of all the priests whom she met in the course of her life, two only, in
the course of a single conversation, had been of any real help to her.
By religious instinct and more or less spontaneously, she went
beyond the distortions caused by fear and the rigorism from which
the Church was then suffering. Without realising the effects of her
struggle, she was to renew the face of God for millions. For the God
of justice and punishment, for hell and the rigour preached within
the Church, she substituted what she saw to be the essence of the
Gospel: hope and trust. This was her great discovery. And what she
rediscovered, i.e. the loving kindness of a God who came down to
earth in the guise of a beggar, she was to live to the last. She didn't
merely talk about it, she carried things further, living this trust to the
last. Thérèse's 'last conversations' with her sisters during her final
six months of life are available in print, in full detail.

Thus Thérèse, of robust constitution, had her first attack of
blood-spitting on Good Friday, 1896. She got over that, but a year
later the tuberculosis had become irreversible and she died by inches
over the next six months. The day she discovered that death was
inevitable, she said: 'The only thing I really wish for now is to love
until I die of love.' This was on 9 June 1897. In July they began
bringing things downstairs in readiness for her burial:

'They had brought her palliasse down (in advance) to display her
on after her death,' one of her sisters relates. 'Thérèse caught sight of
it through the open door and joyfully exclaimed: "Oh, there goes our
palliasse! It will be waiting ready to put my corpse on."

'The candle, holy-water bucket and sprinkler had been put ready
in the room next to the infirmary. She guessed as much and asked for
them to be put where she could see them. She used to look at them
from time to time with evident satisfaction. Smiling, she said, "You
see that candle; when the 'Thief' comes to carry me off, that will be
put in my hand, but you mustn't give me the candlestick—that's far
too ugly!" Then she went over everything that would happen after
she died, happily going into every detail of her burial, using expressions which made us smile when all we wanted was to cry. We
weren't supporting her, she was the one encouraging us.'

But it was the same Thérèse who said at about the same time,
'How is Baby going to face up to dying?' And when someone said,
when she could hardly speak: 'Oh, what a terrible illness! How you
must have suffered!'—'Yes! What a mercy it is to have faith! If I
didn't have faith, I should have killed myself without a moment's
hesitation.'

'What are you up to now? You ought to be trying to go to
sleep.'—'I can't. I'm in too much pain, so I'm praying.'—'And what
are you saying to Jesus?'—'I'm not saying anything, I'm loving
him!'

The temptation to kill herself

And so through the long months the choking fits and haemorrhages
went on—yes, indeed, as for millions of other people, whose sister,
and we might say 'spokesman', she knew herself to be. Then gangrene attacked her intestines. Still Thérèse held firm, though it
didn't stop her from being tempted to kill herself on several occasions.

'Oh, if I didn't have the Faith, I could never endure all this pain.
I'm amazed that atheists don't commit suicide more often.' She
endured the various treatments of the day: blistering, cauterisation,
syrup of slugs, friction with the horse-hair glove (of which she
spiritedly remarked, 'Oh, to be curry-combed as I have been is
worse than anything you can imagine!') Nothing could shake her
trust. 'Oh, how sad life is!' someone said to her. She replied: 'Life's
not sad! Not at all, it's very gay. If you said, "Exile's sad," I could
understand. It's wrong to apply the word life to what has got to
come to an end. The word should only be used for heavenly things,
for what will never die; and then life isn't sad, but gay, very gay!'

Her sister, who was nursing her, asked her to say something nice
to the doctor. 'Oh, dear Mother, that's not my style at all. Let him
think what he likes. I only like simplicity. I hate humbug. Believe
me, what you ask would be wrong for me to do.' She had learnt to
rely on Someone other than herself and was anxious to proclaim her
'secret': 'The little will be judged with extreme mildness. And you
can certainly stay little, even in a very responsible position, even if
you live to be very old. If I had died at the age of eighty, if I had been
to China or all over the world, I should, I am convinced, have died
as little as I am today. And it is written that "at the last, the Lord

will arise to save all the meek and humble on earth". It doesn't say
to *judge*, but to *save*.'

And Thérèse went on making other people laugh, supporting
them, writing and *living*. She had been struggling through the previous eighteen months in the dark night of the soul, no longer feeling
any consolation from her faith. She had truly taken her place at the
table of the hopeless. But one thing remained, absolute: *her trust in
love*. She had given herself to someone who could not possibly let her
down. And her love was to triumph. At the moment of dying, for the
space of a Credo, the darkness was torn aside. She died saying, 'Oh,
I love him. My God, I love you'.

The human being confronting the abyss

Thérèse of Lisieux has been drowned by traditional religious art:
plaster statues and roses. This has given many people an excuse for
not studying the relevance of her life. Now we are better placed to
make an assessment. For example, who were her contemporaries?

She was born at the moment Rimbaud brought out *A Season in
Hell*. Dostoievsky had published *The Rebels* two years before. And
two years later, Nietzsche produced *Human, all too Human*. In that
year, 1873, French society was shaken by four crises: the end of the
Franco-Prussian War, the end of the First Vatican Council, a new
confrontation between Catholics and the State (the birth of the
Third Republic) and the beginning of a new debate between
science and religion (Claude Bernard published the charter of all
modern science in 1878: his *Introduction to the Experimental Method*).
Thus, as the nineteenth century, so quickly relegated to contempt,
drew to its close, we do well to remember that at the very moment
when Thérèse went through her personality change, suddenly discovering her true vocation (what she called her 'conversion') at
Christmas, 1886, when she was thirteen and a half, Freud was staying with Charcot and acquiring the principal insights of Freudian-
ism (the first theory of psychoanalysis dates from 1896, a year after
Thérèse's death); Marx had died three years before; that same year,
1886, Nietzsche published *Beyond Good and Evil* and was preparing
The Antichrist for publication, which came out the same year as
Thérèse entered Carmel (1888). Claudel was converted the same
day as she was, and Charles de Foucauld the same year. And on the
same Christmas Day, 1886, there appeared in the bookshops *The*

Confessions of an Ex-Freethinker by Leo Taxil, an imposter whose career was to affect hers.

Marx, Nietzsche, Freud: the three giants dominating modern thought. With them, the age of roses is over. And in fact the only way of appreciating Thérèse of Lisieux today is by adding her squarely to their company. It is the same battle, all along the line: *man confronting the abyss*. Here lies her genius. Surely one among women who went the farthest, 'to the end'. When she opted for the good, she knew—and says—what it would have been like if she had opted for rupture, loneliness and evil; and when she pursued her quest for God, she knew that it wasn't primarily a case of seeking him, but of his seeking her: 'He will get tired of making me wait for him long before I get tired of waiting for him.'

What is the point of 'saints'?

Ought we to complain about the Church's canonising people 'from the bottom of the pile'? You see, although Thérèse belongs to the heroic line of those who have gone all the way: people like St Augustine, Pascal, Kierkegaard and Dostoievsky, she also belongs to that other group whom the Church has held up as examples since the French Revolution. Whom do we find in this second group? Bernadette of Lourdes, the daughter of a man (wrongly) suspected of being a criminal; Catherine Labouré, an illiterate peasant; the Curé d'Ars; and young Thérèse of Lisieux from the middle classes.

Presumably it is one of the Holy Spirit's ruses to have his message delivered by simple creatures like these. And the same has been said of John XXIII, the farmer's boy made Pope. Will these be the last to be formally canonised, perhaps? Who cares? What matters is that what was previously reserved for privileged beings like Bernard of Clairvaux, Ignatius Loyola or John of the Cross, we now find being offered to everyone: the opportunity of *triumphing over the anguish of our fate*, of triumphing over fear of loneliness in the face of uncertainty over the future and death. And Thérèse it is who reveals the secrets of this democratisation of the 'dark night of the soul' to us. According to her, within us we each have an explosive, infinite strength capable of conquering every fear. This strength, sought by the prophets and great revolutionary figures of her day—and here Thérèse is in complete agreement with them—exists, exists in each of us. We can overcome fear, every fear: fear of the future, fear of our own limitations, fear of others, fear of death, fear of self.

'All you who have toiled and wept, come ... All are called.' There is only one condition on which benefiting from this infinite strength depends: that of accepting the truth about our incapacity and, because of this, of choosing the path of trusting to the last.

Yes, certainly one of the most 'contagiously' loving personalities in human history. It is fitting that, before recognising or working out the theory of women's rights, the Church should have been outflanked, even jolted, by this girl, whose genius we have still not entirely grasped. Thérèse: the memory of a heroic little girl, or message for today? I quote a priest writing from Vietnam in November 1972: 'St Thérèse's centenary, 1973, falls well here, among these remote people. Here in Dalat we have Koho tribesmen, primitive peoples of the High Plateau. The mountain people here are haunted by fear, fear of spirits. Their religion centres on animal blood, to placate the anger of the spirits. To dare, as Thérèse did, to smile at a spirit? To say "our Father" to a spirit? To dedicate oneself to loving a spirit? What a break-through! May the year 1973 bring Heaven's tenderness to the people where we are living. Here, the spirit of the Sun, Siet-Ngkao ("Cut-off-your-head"), the spirit of the Rainbow, Jop-Mham ("Suck-your-blood", like a vampire), the spirit of Thunder, Cong-Co ("Hack-you-in-half"), the spirit of Water, Kuansa ("Claw-you-and-eat-you") and the others are all *against* man. At last Thérèse will tell them of a God who is *on man's side*.'

'Cut-off-your-head', 'Suck-your-blood', 'Claw-you-and-eat-you', class-war, sexuality, daily oppression . . . Don't we all have our own evil 'spirits'? Which of us doesn't need to be delivered from fear? What would be finer than to learn once more to say 'Our Father' with conviction?

3

CHARITY

What kind of appeal can Thérèse of Lisieux have for young people of today? We may as well admit it: our immediate assumption is that this Carmelite of another age must be alien to them. Yet experience proves, when the facts are presented in their true light, that the very opposite is true. Take for instance something that interests even the youngest of us and which can be expressed in one word: the 'collective', i.e., solidarity in life, solidarity in seeking a meaning to life, in working, in sharing. Did Thérèse have a sense of the 'collective'? Unhesitatingly we answer: yes, she did, and more than anyone. But not any old collective. She lived and she died for the greatest collective of them all. Yet the circumstances of her life were such that she might easily have been induced to fall back on her own interests however noble and spiritual they might be, on her own petty preoccupations however apparently virtuous; she might, as we do, very legitimately have stuck to 'a' collective: the one most immediately concerning her, which would have become 'her' collective—her little family, her little convent, her little town, her Church.

That largest collective

But what interested her, and very early in her life too, was that most universal of vocations, a vocation binding her not merely to a little collective, to a project, to an ideal, to a struggle, but to the universe entire. When, exhausted by illness, by fever, she walked the cloisters of Lisieux, she would think about missionaries and offer up her struggle for them. But the collective for which she lived was even larger; her solidarity was not only with her fellow-Christians but— and especially during the last eighteen months of her life—with the hopeless, with atheists, with (to use her own expression) 'materialists'. The people whom she then called her brothers were all those who had lost their bearings, who could no longer find a meaning to their lives. The largest collective of them all, that of the deprived, the lost, the hopeless, the crushed, of the poor all over the world.

For this sense of the collective she had a name, a name commonplace enough but one which she made extraordinarily new. It was *charity*. And here I refer you to what must surely be one of the greatest documents on the topic in human literature, so that you can grasp what it means; I mean the third part of her *Story of a Soul*. It means not merely accepting whatever comes and transforming it into a virtue, into capital, into a treasure to be preserved and defended, but (as St John says) *'living the truth'*. If the revolution which Thérèse operated thereby in the Church could be put into few words, I should say: according to her, everything is given by God, but at the same time everything still has to be done. This was revolutionary. Eighty years before the Second Vatican Council, Thérèse had grasped the radical change of attitude that this requires: charity is a struggle, not fought out merely at the level of ideas, of concepts, but in daily life, in living, and yet this cannot be done except in the name of a love received from on high and transcending us.

If she acts, if she fights, if she goes so far in charity, it is *'in response to Someone's good pleasure'*, as she constantly affirms, to the good pleasure of Someone who loves her. And this, in the commonplace routine of everyday life. By becoming incarnate, God consented to be commonplace, and Thérèse reminds us of the infinite grandeur of the commonplace. For her, this was the *second conversion*, the most important one, offered to every Christian, which consists of refusing to allow there to be any gap in life between what we say and what we do.

Everything is given, everything has still got to be done

Thérèse had made a habit of smiling whenever her work was interrupted by a nun's coming, whether with or without good reason, to ask for help. She mentions this humorously in her last manuscript. We, on the other hand, in similar circumstances are tempted gently to intimate to the person asking for help that we are doing them a favour. Thérèse did not yield to this temptation; she was not the mistress of her own time. At the beginning of any free period she prepared herself to be disturbed; thus, she says, nothing ever took her by surprise; she was ready to be disturbed: 'I want to be, I count on being. . . . And so I am always happy.'

The time is now mid-June, 1897. For the past eight days she has known for certain that her illness cannot be cured. Straining her strength to the utmost, she sometimes takes more than half an hour to climb the stairs to the floor where her cell is. Exhausted by fever she forces herself by obedience to write the continuation of her life-story. When put in the garden in the invalid chair previously used by her paralysed father: 'Sometimes I would be writing about charity and very often someone would come and interrupt me; then I would try not to be impatient, and to practise what I was writing.' 'As soon as I take up my pen, along comes one of the nuns with her fork on her shoulder. She thinks it will amuse me if she has a little chat. Hay, ducks, chicken, the doctor's visit: all is grist to the mill. Admittedly this doesn't last long, but there's more than one charitable nun and suddenly another hay-maker lays a few flowers in my lap, possibly thinking to inspire me with poetic thoughts. But poetic thoughts are not what I'm wanting just now and I should have preferred the flowers to stay swaying on their stalks. Eventually, tired of opening and shutting my wretched exercise-book, I open another book (which won't stay open) and say resolutely that I'm copying out thoughts from the Psalms and Gospel for our Superior's birthday. And this is true enough, since I don't stint the quotations. . . . Beloved Mother, I'm sure I should make you laugh if I told you about all my adventures in the groves of Carmel. I doubt if I can have written ten lines without being interrupted. This wouldn't normally have made me laugh or even amused me, but for love of God and my sisters (who are so kind to me) I try to look happy and above all to be so. . . . There! you see! there goes another haymaker, who has just said, "Poor little sister, you must find it tiring, writing all day like that." "Don't worry," I said, "I look as if I'm writing a lot, but really I've hardly written a thing." "Oh, good!" she said, looking reassured, "but all the same, I'm very glad we're haymaking. It makes a little bit of distraction for you." The fact is, it's a very big distraction.'

Being very sensitive herself, she knew from personal experience how upsetting a tactless or unfriendly remark could be. When her father's illness affected his brain, there were plenty of these. Behind these agonising shafts, these 'pin-pricks' as she called them, Thérèse allowed herself to see only 'the gentle hand of her Jesus'. And she knew that the least of her sufferings, offered up in love, could save a soul.

Thérèse knew that the first thing about living the Gospel is that we have to do it with our nearest neighbour, with someone whom we ourselves have not chosen. She was careful not to stop short at external appearances. She quickly realised that, in community, dislikes are often caused by the fact that people allow themselves to be mesmerised by the more obvious faults of those around them, instead of making an effort to discover their good qualities. 'There is,' she wrote, 'in the community one sister who has the gift of displeasing me whatever she does. I found her ways, her words, her character, all very disagreeable. And yet she is a holy religious who must be very acceptable to God; so, not wishing to give way to the natural dislike which I felt, I told myself that charity should not consist in feelings, but in works. I then set myself to doing for this sister what I would have done for the person whom I love best. Each time I met her I prayed to God for her, offering up all her virtues and merits. I knew that this was pleasing to Jesus.'

Here we have Thérèse at grips with dislike, and her immediate reaction is a positive one. Not content with resisting her antipathy to a nun whose character was somewhat 'rigid' and extremely irritating to her, she decided that the nun in question must have qualities and merits known to God alone. We proceed: 'I wasn't content with praying a lot for the nun who caused me so many struggles, I tried to do everything I could for her and, whenever I was tempted to answer her disagreeably, I gave her my sweetest smile instead and tried to change the subject. . . . Often meeting this nun in the course of my work, whenever my struggles became too violent, I would quit the field. As she never had the slightest inkling of my feelings about her, she never suspected what the motives were for my behaviour and is still convinced that I like her very much. One day at recreation she said to me, looking very pleased, "Sister Thérèse of the Child Jesus, would you mind telling me what you find so attractive about me? Whenever you look at me, I see you smile." What attracted me [Thérèse comments] was Jesus hidden in the depths of her soul.' Charity, the collective: a giant's battle in a day-to-day routine, but inspired by another love than ours.

And to put the finishing touches to what Thérèse wrote in *The Story of a Soul*, here is the statement made by her elder sister Marie at the Process for canonisation. This is how the story ends: 'She concealed her dislike so well that, under the impression that she liked this particular nun very much, I felt rather jealous and said to her one day, "I can't help telling you one thing that upsets me.... It seems to me that you like Sister Thérèse of St Augustine better than me. And I don't think this is right, since God created family ties when all's said and done. But you always seem so pleased to see her that I can't draw any other conclusion, since you never seem anything like so pleased to be with me." She laughed good-naturedly but never gave me the slightest hint about the dislike which this religious inspired in her.' Consider this laugh and this silence. An indiscretion thirty years after Thérèse's death was responsible for the nun's discovering that she was the religious in question in *The Story of a Soul*. All the other nuns in the convent had guessed long ago, but she had never recognised herself, remaining convinced that she had always been a consolation to the saint. But one day Canon Travert, chaplain to the nuns, irritated beyond measure by the said religious, told her in a fit of bad temper that it had been she all along. Yes, the unlimited grandeur of the ordinary where, every day, 'the truth' has 'to be lived'. It seems very simple in the telling, but what strength and courage it takes!

In the last months of her life, she acquired an even better understanding of the demands and importance of the second commandment: 'I understood what it meant before, of course ... but I hadn't grasped the inner meaning of Jesus's words, "The second commandment is like the first". For He means that we should not merely love our neighbour as much as we love ourselves, but should love him as much as He, Jesus, loves him and will go on loving him to the end of the world.' Then, far from finding this programme impossible, Thérèse adds: 'Oh, Lord, I know that you never command the impossible. You know my weakness better than I.... You know very well that I could never love my sisters in religion as much as you love them, if you, my Jesus, did not keep loving them in me.... Oh, how I love this new commandment, since it assures me that your will is to love—in me—all those whom you command me to love!' Thérèse concludes: 'Love alone is what counts.' 'For me to love you as much as you love me, I shall have to borrow your love; then alone shall I find repose.'

A second conversion

Being a Christian means consenting to a second conversion: like St
Peter after his betrayal, like St Paul, St Augustine, St Francis, Joan
of Arc and so on. And Thérèse shows us clearly and simply what the
laws are governing this. One day, it becomes no longer enough to
profess a system of satisfying ideals, not even enough to proclaim
them, to tell them to other people, to preach them, to discuss this or
that change in life or Church, to take sides in the debate between
prayer and politics. Beyond this, there is another conversion offered
us, a second conversion: to follow Someone to the end, to be ready to
burn our boats, to take a path where it is no longer a matter of opting
for Christ and Christianity, but of preferring it. Yes, of preferring it,
not merely choosing it. First conversions can be violent, though
exciting. The second type often seem impossible. Yet there is no
Christianity without the second. This is where Thérèse of Lisieux's
complete revolution begins: living the truth in everyday life, but in
the name of a love coming from on high and hence transcending all
our petty limitations, petty evasions and petty revenges. Thérèse
understood this and willed it to the end. Countless anecdotes illustrate her fantastic powers of concentration on living the truth in the
opportunities offered by the commonplace.

   In her very simple, very direct sort of life, Thérèse made the same
reversal of priorities as the Second Vatican Council was later to
make, the emphasis falling rather on the way you live than the way
you think. She believed that God appears in the events of every day,
a God present and saying to each individual, 'Are you willing'—
'Nothing upsets me,' she said, 'nothing destroys my plans. Nothing
at all.' Compare this with the words of *Lumen Gentium* issued by the
Second Vatican Council: 'Accordingly all Christians, in the conditions, duties and circumstances of their life and through all these,
will sanctify themselves more and more if they receive all things with
faith from the hand of the heavenly Father and cooperate with the
divine will, thus showing forth in that temporal service the love with
which God has loved the world.' And the contemporary writer J.
Loew comments: 'Whatever happens comes to me literally as a
present from God, a present in the double sense of presence and gift.
The present moment comes to me in the form of an action offered me
or asked of me. Whether making my bed or celebrating mass, clean-
ing the vegetables or making my communion, waiting for the bus or
saying my prayers, at that moment the action offered me is the
presence which God is taking in my life' *(Comme s'il voyait l'invisible)*.

Cold water and the Christmas tree

There are many practical examples to show how charity imposed a unity on Thérèse's life and how exactly she knew how *simultaneously* to renounce her own will, love others and respond to God. These three aspects of charity come in ascending order of merit and only together provide the dynamism for love to be carried to the limits and beyond, loyal to the last.

One of Thérèse's novices, the one whom she probably loved most, almost certainly the liveliest of her companions, a Parisian and a wag, recorded many incidents concerning her. Her testimony given at the Process is particularly valuable and telling. 'One day I asked her which was better: to go and rinse things at the cold-water tap or to stay and wash them out with hot water in the laundry. She replied, "Oh, that's an easy question! When it costs you an effort to go to the cold tap, that means it must cost others an effort too; so go! If, on the other hand, the weather's hot, stay for preference in the laundry. By taking the worst places, you practise self-mortification and at the same time charity for others, since you leave them the better ones." After that, I realised why I used to see her go to the laundry when the weather was hot and more particularly to the most airless parts of it! I witnessed her heroic acts of charity in connexion with the holy religious mentioned in her Life who had the knack of displeasing her whatever she did. She used to lavish so much attention and affection on her that you might have thought it a particular friendship.'

We might recall two other stories here as far transcending their commonplace externals. An elderly nun was allergic to the scent of flowers. Someone made the convent a present of some artificial ones and Thérèse put them by the statue in the cloister. Coming out of chapel, she noticed the old nun make an irritable little gesture. What should we have done in the circumstances? The normal reaction would have been to get a rise out of her by letting her make a fuss and make herself look silly. With a little more virtue, we might have explained that there was nothing to be worried about because the flowers weren't real. Thérèse immediately grasped the situation and with absolute and instant realism intervened before anything could happen, by saying, 'Oh, Mother, do look how well people can imitate nature now. . . .' In a word, Thérèse had been 'neighbourly', had recognised who her neighbour was.

On another occasion, it was to do with getting the Christmas tree through the garden gate of the convent. The sister portress couldn't manage on her own and during recreation—'not a very cheerful recreation,' Thérèse noted—came to ask Thérèse to give a hand. Thérèse knew that the nun sitting next to her was desperately anxious for a change. So—stratagem—Thérèse folded her sewing up very slowly, giving the nun next to her time to get to her feet. The portress said something like this: 'It's clear, Sister Thérèse, that you're in no hurry to help.' What should we have done? With a little virtue and a little forethought—we could have shown ourselves off to advantage: 'Dear Sister So-and-so, it will do you good. You go instead of me, it will make a nice change for you.' With a little more virtue, we might have hit on the same stratagem but, at the portress's retort—at the rebuke publicly administered—we should have protested. Thérèse said nothing. She was later to comment, and here lies the nub: 'Since then, I have never again dared pass judgement on anyone.'

A 'political' dimension?

Cynics may write off the foregoing as edifying convent twaddle. But when someone leads a life never deviating from such absolute silence and concentration it is so extraordinary, such a victory over self, that it testifies to a strength much greater than our own: in a word, to God's. And if this explanation still strikes us as hackneyed, it means that we still haven't become aware how cruel and bewildering the simplicity of the commonplace can be. Not Thérèse however: that master of charity, master and exemplar of the second conversion, alien to all forms of deceit with her pitiless yet sweet lucidity— infinitely sweet since expressing the tenderness of God himself.

One of her biographers, seeking out her limitations (and certainly she had some) emphasises that 'Thérèse had no political dimension'. True, she did not practise politics, but this doesn't mean that her life had no political dimension.

Indeed, wouldn't it be the greatest of political victories—and I mean political in its normal sense—for a Christian today to achieve her victorious charity: that is, a charity refusing to classify or to contrast people as 'good' or 'bad', thus repudiating the deadly malady of people at large and Christians in particular, known as Manichaeism—the refusal to believe that good and evil exist in parallel or that any evil can ultimately escape the effects of love? Thérèse's revolution is to have proved that the opposite is true and to show us that every one of us can practise this victorious charity in everyday life. There are no 'bad' people who can ultimately escape victorious charity, God's victory. There are no 'bad people to be eliminated'. For a Christian, for Thérèse, love alone in the final event will triumph, over all strife between classes, interests or groups. The communion of saints, the 'collective', is possible: the collective arising from God's victory, called 'charity'. 'Lord, your child asks you to forgive her brothers, she consents to eat the bread of sorrow as long as you wish and has no desire to leave this table, laden with bitterness, at which poor sinners eat, until the day you choose. May all not yet enlightened by the luminous torch of the Faith eventually see its light. O Jesus, if the table soiled by them has to be purified by a soul who loves you, I am more than happy to eat the bread of trial until you are pleased to admit me to your kingdom of light.'

4

THE FORCE OF SILENCE

The flautist in the orchestra

In the old days, my community had a great sense of fun. Birthdays and anniversaries were celebrated with happy regularity. Practical jokes spared neither procurator nor superior. They were the product of shared affection and of a very wise tradition. Then came the age of questioning and the period of the so-called social sciences: such 'bourgeois' entertainments had to stop. Superiors took fright. The result: moroseness. No more guitars, no more cigars. Now it will take years to invent a new art of life.

Life was not boring in the Carmelite convent at Lisieux. Thérèse had been as deeply happy in religious as in family life. She always emphasised this. More than fifty times in *The Story of a Soul* she applies the word 'happy' to herself. Along with happiness, joy and pleasure, it is one of the most frequently used words in her *Letters* and in her *Last Conversations*.

If, in the orchestra of the sons of God, Philip Neri and Thomas Moore—those princes of humour and good-nature—play trumpet and double-bass, Thérèse of Lisieux and Francis of Assisi undoubtedly play the flute or oboe: precise, clear, unexpected, never wounding to the ear.

It is, I suppose, impossible for anyone not having led the religious life before 1950 to imagine the degree to which a community of this sort (in which the way of life, depending on the religious order involved, had varied so little over the previous three to seven centuries) could follow a penitential rule of incredible rigour (cold, sleep, fasting) and simultaneously enjoy a happy sense of community. I don't imagine people have ever laughed so heartily as they used to laugh in convents. 'Mystical, comical: everything by turns.' We must not overlook Thérèse's sense of humour. It could have been cruel to others. It never was. Though it was remorselessly so to herself. One day someone will have to analyse how much she owed here to her father. Their relationship was in one respect that of 'a double act'. Thérèse was very good at impersonations. 'She has a particular gift for mimicking the tone of voice and mannerisms of other people', Léonie was to state at the Process. For us, this sense of humour is by no means of secondary interest: in charity, it expresses the rigour and force of truth. Thérèse's bursts of laughter are what ✦ set her free, and will always set her free from the activities of sugar-icing mixers and plaster-statue-makers on the one hand, and the theories of psycho-historical theologisers regularly closing in on her on the other. By her strength in tenderness, by the extraordinary in the ordinary, we can all trace the outlines of a sanctity possible also for ourselves.

The democratisation of holiness

Francis of Assisi would probably have made a first-rate spiritual director-general: the history of his order goes to show this. You can't expect everyone to be everything. Thérèse didn't have all the necessary qualities for that, and she certainly had her limitations. We may justifiably ask, for instance, whether she had a sufficient love of life.

This is where her sense of humour seems so important. In her case, as we have said, it was the product of a rigorous yet tender regard for truth, of an awareness of limitations but without false indulgence, the patience of the little way and the acceptance of no longer being her own master. Thérèse had chosen not to tread the 'heights', not to practise the aristocratic type of spirituality deriving from a misconception of Bérulle and then influencing her convent. Her mentality was quite opposite and she stayed bravely loyal to her own intuition, the views of some of the other nuns notwithstanding. Very likely she got this taste for self-effacement and tenacity from her mother Zélie Martin, though Thérèse transformed it into the hidden mainspring of her whole life: she consented to being 'nothing', to being regarded as 'nothing' and to knowing herself to ⌐ be regarded as such. 'By clinging to faithfulness in little things—the favoured ground of the poor, the simple, the realistic—she rescues holiness from the prejudice surrounding it' (C. De Meester 'Actualité de Thérèse de Lisieux', *Carmel*, no. 16). She did not set store by things apparently extraordinary, by 'startling deeds' as she called them—this was not her little way. She did indeed set holiness free. Speaking of democratisation, we might quote Thomas Merton: 'St Thérèse's little way is an explicit rejection of any exalted or sublime notion tending to cut man off from his ordinary existence or to divide him into halves, one half entrusted to the angels, the other roaming in this vale of tears' (Introduction to *The Way of Chuang Tzu*).

Her great method was silence

'All too late, experience has taught me that we should not evaluate people by their vices, but contrariwise by what they have kept intact and pure, by what there is still left in them of childhood, however deep we have to search for it' (Bernanos, *Lettre aux Anglais*).

We don't have to go down very far to see how Thérèse's virtue can and still does have a liberating effect. After the first Process for her beatification in 1910, people wondered whether she had suffered enough. In contrast, at the second Process in 1915-17, we see the wretched nuns falling over themselves to emphasise Thérèse's sufferings, Mother Marie de Gonzague's lack of understanding and so forth. Where we are concerned, Thérèse did even better, and more simply too.

It has been said of St Thomas Aquinas that he knew how to become a saint without being a bore to other people. Thérèse's virtue would certainly be a bore if it were primarily of the order of exceptional suffering or of spiritual instruction. But it is of the everyday order: simple, realistic, a gamble, crude and sometimes cruel, and within everyone's reach.

Her fellow-nuns were perfectly right about this. 'At the beginning of her illness, she used to have to take medicine a few minutes before meals. One old nun was shocked at this and complained on the grounds that it was an infringement of the rule. Sister Thérèse of the Child Jesus would only have had to say a word or two to justify herself and pacify the nun in question. She forbore to do so, modelling her conduct on that of the Blessed Virgin who preferred to let herself be defamed rather than justify herself to St Joseph . . . She would often speak to me about the Virgin's behaviour. Like Mary's, her great method was silence. This reserve was her strength and the basis of her perfection' (Sr Geneviève). 'What treasures we should win in religious life, were we to do as Thérèse did: bear all and say nothing!' (Sr Marie of the Sacred Heart).

She herself constantly reverted to this and is very clear on the topic. It is very simple, always unexpected, as varied as the conditions of daily life: to learn never to defend oneself, never to justify oneself, never to judge hastily, always to respect confidences, rather die than speak. 'When we are misunderstood and misjudged, what is the point of defending ourselves or explaining? We should let the matter drop and say nothing; it is so lovely to say nothing and allow ourselves to be judged for good or ill! We don't find anywhere in the Gospel that Mary Magdalen offered explanations when her sister accused her of doing nothing, sitting at Jesus's feet. She didn't say, "Oh, Martha, if only you knew how happy I am! If only you were hearing what I can hear! And anyhow, Jesus himself has told me to stay here!"—No, she chose to say nothing. Oh, blessed the silence that gives such peace to the soul!' 'Oh, there are very few perfect religious who don't on occasion do things in a slap-dash way, thinking, "I don't much care for this. . . . There's no harm in talking here, in doing as I think there. . . ." How rare, the ones who always do the best they can! Yet these are the ones who are happiest. It is the same with silence too. What good it does the soul, what defects in charity it prevents, as well as all sorts of other difficulties! I particularly mention silence, since this is where we fall short most of all.' 'When you are very sick in body, everyone does their best to look after you; if it's something wrong with your chest, they shut out the draughts and the nurse is there to see you have everything you want. Oh, why don't we do the same for our sisters' spiritual illnesses? This is what God asks of me and, if I get better, this is what I shall go on doing with all my heart. If a nun is spiritually sick, unpleasing in every respect, other people avoid her, look askance at her and, instead of trying to look after her, sometimes say wounding things which she has neither the strength nor ability to bear! When really it's the healthy ones who ought to be treated like that, since they, being fit, could happily endure being humiliated, despised and forsaken. So you see, I intend to reserve my smiles, my affection and my attentions for the sick ones. That is what I consider to be true charity.' We might add one further telling reflection; when Thérèse fell sick herself, she said: 'Dear sisters, pray for the mortally sick poor. If you only knew what it felt like! How little it takes to lose patience! We must be charitable to everyone. I wouldn't have believed it, before.'

Thérèse said it and proved it. 'When she entered Carmel, I have to admit there was an undue tendency to laxness. Several religious did of course keep the rule properly, but there were others, and a considerable number, who did in fact abuse it. The Servant of God applied herself to her duty without bothering about what others might be doing; I never once saw her linger with the groups of nuns who used to gather round the Mother Prioress to hear the news when she came out of the parlour; nor listen to breaches of charity. In our great family sorrows, she was much more courageous than we were. After we had been in the parlour, for instance, and heard the very sad news about our father's state of health, instead of cheering herself up by talking to us, she immediately resumed her duties in the community' (Mother Agnes).

'When, for instance, in refectory someone forgot to serve her, she was pleased and would not draw attention to it. She would say, "I am like one of the truly poor. There's no point in taking a vow of poverty, if you don't intend to suffer the effects." Sometimes a nun would pass off as her own something Thérèse had said. She found this quite natural and used to say that, by virtue of poverty, she had no more right to this particular possession than to any other one' (Mother Agnes). 'The Servant of God was faithful in controlling her temper ... Although she had a very lively imagination, she never showed off ... She advised me never to tell her about anything that had upset me while I was still disturbed. She would say, "When you are describing an interior conflict, even to Reverend Mother, never do it with the aim of having the nun rebuked who provoked it or of having the cause of complaint put right; but speak with complete detachment. If you do not feel detached and there is still so much as a spark of passion in your heart, it is more perfect to say nothing and wait ... since speaking in these circumstances often only makes matters worse." She always practised this advice in her own behaviour; never was she seen to run to Reverend Mother in the heat of battle; she always waited until she was mistress of herself' (Sr Geneviève). Her elder sister, Marie, found this almost shocking: 'It is unusual to see the same invariable equanimity, the same smile forever on someone's lips ... even during her worst ordeals. Consequently I had no idea how much she was suffering, in her great temptations against faith for instance, until I read her manuscript after she was dead' (Sr Marie of the Sacred Heart).

The strength to resist

Sr Geneviève writes: 'I was thirteen years old when my father told me that he was going to have me taught drawing. Thérèse was present too at the time and I could see her eyes light up with envy, hoping against hope that my father would say that she could learn too. What he said was, "Now, my little queen, how would you like to have drawing lessons?" She was just going to answer when Marie spoke up and said that the house was already full of "daubs" which needed framing. Marie carried the day. Thérèse said nothing. No one had any idea what she was going through. But later, recalling the incident a few weeks before she died, she confessed to me that she had felt so violent a desire to expostulate that she still wondered after all those years how she had ever had the strength to resist.'

'From the moment she entered our Carmel—although she was only fifteen—she was treated less than gently. She was given the stalest leftovers to eat. We used to say in the kitchen, "No one's going to eat that, let's give it to Sister Thérèse of the Child Jesus. She never refuses anything." And so, right to the end of the week, you would see omelette or herring keep turning up on her plate, though cooked the previous Sunday. In refectory, she and the nun sitting next to her were supposed to share a bottle of cider so small that it hardly held two glassfuls. Consequently she drank none, so as not to deprive her neighbour. She could have taken water from the water-jug, but abstained so that no one would notice. Three days before she died, though tortured by fever, she refrained from asking for water, into which we used to put a few bits of ice; she also refrained from asking for the grapes when these were thoughtlessly left out of her reach. Seeing her look at her glass, I realised that she was mortifying herself and said, "Would you like some iced water?" She replied, "Yes, I would very much." I then said, "But Reverend Mother has ordered you to ask for whatever you need; so, under obedience, do so." She said, "I do ask for what I need. But when I haven't any grapes, I don't ask." She never claimed anything back that was taken away from her. She even allowed others to rob her, you might say, of the intellectual gifts which God had so liberally bestowed on her; for, in recreation, if people took advantage of her witty remarks to repeat them as of their own invention, she would willingly let them have the honour of amusing others, without revealing their real origin' (Sr Marie of the Sacred Heart).

'One winter's evening at the beginning of 1895, two and a half years before Sister Thérèse died, I was with my two sisters (Marie and Thérèse) when Sister Thérèse of the Child Jesus was telling me about certain incidents in her childhood. Sister Marie of the Sacred Heart (my elder sister Marie) said to me, "Oh, Mother, what a pity not to have all this down on paper! If you were to ask Sister Thérèse

of the Child Jesus to write her childhood memories for us, how nice
that would be!" "What an excellent idea!" I replied and, turning to
Sister Thérèse of the Child Jesus who was laughing as though we
were making fun of her, I said, "I order you to write me everything
you can remember about your childhood." The Servant of God set
to work under obedience, since I was her Mother Prioress. She wrote
only during her free time and gave me her exercise-book on 20
January, 1896 for my birthday. I was at evening prayers. Passing me
on her way to her stall, Sister Thérèse of the Child Jesus knelt down
and handed me this treasure. I acknowledged it with a simple nod
and put the manuscript on our stall without opening it. I did not
have occasion to read it until after the elections in the spring of that
same year. I noticed the virtue of the Servant of God for, after her act
of obedience, she did not bother her head about it again. She never
asked me if I had read her book, nor what I thought of it. One day
when I told her I hadn't had time to read any of it, she did not seem
the least put out' (Mother Agnes).

'It was noticed that in recreation she never spoke first, never gave
her opinion unless it was asked for. And yet, with her quick mind,
what witty, penetrating retorts must often have sprung to her lips! In
the parlour, she showed the same discretion, so much so that even in
the family circle people used to say that Thérèse had no personality;
or rather, she went ignored. We used to say that, having entered the
convent too young, her education had been cut short and that this
would affect her for the rest of her life' (Sr Geneviève).

'In the last days of her life (this was in high summer), when she
was burning with fever, I wanted to take the sheet off her feet to
make her cooler, but she said, "Perhaps this isn't allowed?" Mother
Marie de Gonzague had told us some time before that even in summer it was better to keep our blankets on, and Sister Thérèse of the
Child Jesus did not consider herself dispensed by illness from practising obedience and mortification. One word from her would have
got her the relief which all sick people take as a matter of course,
without so much as imagining they need permission' (Sr Marie of
the Sacred Heart).

'Suppose Reverend Mother were to throw it on the fire?'

At the first Process, Mother Agnes deposed: 'She also said, "Once I
am dead, the manuscript (her life-story) should be printed without

delay." I said, "So you think you will do good to souls by means of the manuscript?"—"Yes, it's an instrument which God will use to answer my prayers. It will do good to all sorts of souls, except recipients of exceptional graces."—"But," I went on, "suppose Reverend Mother were to throw it on the fire?"—"Well, I still shouldn't have the least worry or the least doubt about my mission. I should simply think that God was going to answer my prayers by other means".'

Mother Agnes again: 'We had been having an intimate conversation about the little importance often attached to hidden virtue. (Thérèse replied:) "That is what struck me about the Life of our Father St. John of the Cross, when they used to say: Brother John of the Cross? Why he's a less than ordinary religious!" '

Mother Agnes: 'We only realised towards the end of her life that the cold—no doubt owing to the state of her health—was a particularly painful ordeal for her. Never however was she seen to rub her hands in winter or adopt an attitude giving the least hint of her suffering. She never said, "It's very cold" or "It's hot". She never complained about anything. One day one of the nuns, trying to fix the Servant of God's scapular, ran the pin through the material and through her skin as well. Sister Thérèse of the Child Jesus gave no sign and cheerfully went on with her work in the refectory for several hours. In the end, however, she became nervous, she said, "that she might not be practising obedience" . . . and pulled the pin out of her shoulder.'

Sister Marie of the Trinity deposed at the first Process: 'One day I had a violent headache and Sister Thérèse of the Child Jesus wanted me to go and tell Reverend Mother. When I demurred, saying that it would be a way of asking for sympathy, she said to me, "What would you say if you had the same obligation imposed on you as I had when I was a postulant and novice? Our novice-mistress ordered me to tell her whenever I had a stomach-ache. Since I had one every day, this order was an absolute torture to me. Whenever the stomach-ache came on, I would rather have taken a good hiding than go and tell her; but under obedience I did tell her each time. Having forgotten the order she had given me, the novice-mistress used to say, "Poor child, your health will never allow you to keep the Rule, it's too much of a strain for you!" Or she would ask Mother Marie de Gonzague for medicine for me. At which the latter would show her displeasure by saying, "Good heavens, that girl is always complaining! We come to Carmel to suffer; if she can't bear her woes, why doesn't she leave?" Even so, I went on confessing my

stomach-aches under obedience for a long, long time, at the risk of
being sent away—until eventually God, taking pity on my weakness,
granted me the favour of being discharged from the obligation of
having to tell her this.'

'I wouldn't have raised a finger'

In January 1896, Mother Marie de Gonzague had 'begun a cam-
paign to have Sister Geneviève sent to the Carmel at Saigon' and
had tried to postpone the date of her profession 'for reasons of
jealousy'. Thérèse did not hesitate to protest: 'There are kinds of
ordeal which ought never to be used.' This gesture was later to be
mentioned in her Process.

On 2 August, 1896, when the departure of Mother Agnes for a
Carmel in the missions was under discussion, the situation was quite
different. Thérèse explains: 'I had not only assented to being exiled
among an unknown people but—which was much harder for me—I
also assented to my sisters' being exiled. I shall never forget 2
August, 1896, the day when the missionaries actually left and when
there was a serious possibility that Mother Agnes of Jesus might
have gone too. I wouldn't have raised a finger to stop her going but I
felt desperately sad at heart. Jesus said nothing, he would not calm
the tempest. And I kept saying to him, "My God, for love of you I
accept all. If you wish it, I am ready to suffer until I die of grief."
Jesus was satisfied with my assent. But a few months later, the
departure of Sister Geneviève and Sister Marie of the Trinity was
also mooted; and then I suffered in quite a different way, though
very intimately and very deeply. I kept thinking of all the trials and
disappointments which they would have to endure. My sky was
black with clouds, yet the depths of my heart remained calm and at
peace.'

She never abandoned this resolute attitude of mind, especially as
regards her sisters: 'We must pay particular attention to keeping the
Rule. After being in the parlour, don't stop and talk among your-
selves, for that is like being at home and you're not depriving your-
selves of anything.' And: 'When I am gone, take care not to start
leading family life, not to repeat without permission what has been
said in parlour, and furthermore not to ask permission unless something useful is involved.' She was herself extremely careful about
this, even though it meant grieving her sister, Mother Agnes; she

told her nothing about her early haemorrhages for fourteen months. She had informed her Prioress and that was enough; similarly, for two years, she told her nothing about Father Roulland, a missionary priest who had been entrusted to her as her spiritual brother; her ordeal of faith was similarly to be concealed from her sisters.

Then, two months before she died, when things were at their worst on 29 July, she was to have the right to speak out. A nun had repeated something to her which had been said in recreation: 'Why do people talk about Sister Thérèse of the Child Jesus as though she were a saint? True, she has practised virtue, but this wasn't virtue acquired through humiliations and least of all through suffering.' Thérèse then said to Mother Agnes, 'And when you think what I have suffered since earliest childhood! It's good for me at the point of death to see what a poor opinion creatures have of me' (Mother Agnes).

Her discretion was such that it seemed natural to her character, even in moments of crisis. On Sunday morning, 29 July, 1894, a telegram conveyed the news to Lisieux that Monsieur Martin had died at La Musse. 'That afternoon,' Sister Marie of the Sacred Heart was later to relate, 'Madame Maudelonde asked to see us in the parlour. I can still see poor little Thérèse. She was pale and followed us in without a word. In the parlour she hardly said anything either, that was her way, and no one paid any attention to her, since she was the youngest.'

'You will be sent away.' 'Yes, I know.'

Saying nothing, having such esteem for oneself as to let others take pride of place, isn't the same as not daring to speak up when one ought to. One incident is enough to illustrate this. The date is the end of 1892. Of the three youngest members of the community, Thérèse was the sacristan and Sisters Marie-Madeleine and Marthe were the cooks. The last named, who was jolly but rather stupid, had become unduly attached to the Mother Prioress, Mother Marie de Gonzague, 'like a dog to its master'. In *The Story of a Soul*, Thérèse relates how on 8 December, she made up her mind to do her duty as novice-mistress and explain to Sister Marthe that her attachment was excessive. What however she does not relate is related by her sister Agnes, i.e. the risk that Thérèse was taking that day. Thérèse 'had decided to open the eyes of her companion, who was being too attentive to Mother Marie de Gonzague'. She weighed up the risks involved in doing so and then took Sister Agnes of Jesus into her confidence. 'I can still see her that evening in the sacristy,' the latter was to testify. ' "Pray hard for me," she said in a serious tone. "The Blessed Virgin has inspired me to explain matters to Sister Marthe. Tonight I am going to tell her just what I think about her." I said, "But you run the risk of having your words repeated and then Reverend Mother won't be able to bear the sight of you and you will be sent away to another convent." "Yes, I know," she replied, "but since I'm now sure that it's my duty to speak, I can't let the possible consequences deter me." '

For her, silence was never to be purchased at the price of truth. Her *Last Conversations* give numerous proofs of this, always with that touch of humour with which she assented to being no more than she was. 'Sister Marie of the Sacred Heart said to her that the angels would accompany our Lord to attend her death-bed, and that she would see them in all their radiant beauty. "Such pictures say nothing to me. I can only thrive on truth. This is why I have never desired to have visions. On earth, you can't see heaven or the angels as they are. I would rather wait until I'm dead." ' And again: 'When I think, all my life how hard I've always found it to say the rosary!' She had it in her to say: 'It isn't as bad as it looks [dying of love] provided you can actually do it.' And: 'I tell the whole truth; if people don't want to hear it, they shouldn't ask me.' And: 'O my God, I truly want to hear you. I beg you, answer me when I humbly say, What is the truth? Let me see things as they are, let nothing blind me to it!' And on the day she died: 'I have only ever sought the truth.' How impressive this is!

'For a long while at evening meditation, my place used to be in front of a nun who had a curious quirk and who, I think, must have been an exceptional soul—for she hardly ever used a book. That was how I noticed! As soon as this nun came in, she used to begin making a funny little noise which sounded like two shells being rubbed together. I was the only person to notice this, since I have very acute hearing (a bit too acute, sometimes). I can't tell you, Mother, how tiresome I found this little noise. I longed to turn round and look at the person who was making it and who was obviously unaware of her mannerism. It was the only way of bringing it to her notice. But deep in my heart I felt it would be better to endure this for love of God and not upset the nun. So I kept still. I tried to unite myself to God and forget the little noise. It was quite useless, I could feel the sweat breaking out and was forced merely to make a prayer of suffering, but while I was suffering I tried not to pray in an irritable way, but joyfully and peacefully, at least in my inner soul. I then did my best to love the horrid little noise. Instead of trying not to hear it—which couldn't be done—I concentrated on listening to it as though it were a magnificent concert, and my entire meditation was spent in offering this concert to Jesus.'

Those no longer able to speak

To sum up all those anecdotes and indicate what most shows the simplicity, greatness, realism and practical intelligence inherent in Thérèse's virtue, four words are enough: the force of silence. Silence, which is within everybody's reach, is surely the best way of expressing both love and strength—like the silence of Christ and the Virgin at Nazareth. To begin with, this may be attributed to all sorts of different motives: practice, devotion, obedience, spiritual prowess. Never mind. If this is kept up for a lifetime, it must be recognised as coming from another type of love. Someone else had traced the path, Thérèse was doing her best to imitate him. But she was led even further: at this third stage, it was no longer a matter of self-mortification, nor even of imitating Christ but, by force of humiliations, of just consenting to join the category of the deprived, of those no longer able to speak. She knew the description of the Suffering Servant in Isaiah 53 by heart. What she had read, she saw come to pass in her father, then in herself. She perceived the meaning and vast scope of this: not only an invitation to imitate the hidden life of Nazareth, but a call to be united with him who all his life kept silent about his divinity and experienced humiliation to the point of being put to death like a slave.

Thus, for her, silence not only manifests the presence of charity permeating her day-to-day life and all her 'virtues' but also shows that hope is the fairest fruit of charity in any life. This is why we shall deal with hope after charity. For Thérèse, silence became what in the cruellest of circumstances best revealed how determined she was to leave the initiative to God. It was this absence of personal intervention 'to put things right' which Thérèse admired in the Virgin (her silence with regard to Joseph, for instance). As though silence alone could tell God, 'It's up to you'. Silence becomes all powerful, since it shows that, accepting our own limitations completely and by saying nothing, we go on hoping all the same, like Daniel (3:17-18), like Job, like all those faced with God's silence. This is the moment of the 'impossible step', of the last circle—hope. And for Thérèse, it seemed, God was not prepared to act, in the short term. She therefore consented to enter the silence of the Suffering Servant who called for help 'with violent clamour and tears' (Hebr. 5:7) and was heard. 'Your strength will lie in silence and hope', says the Carmelite Rule.

5

THE IMPOSSIBLE STEP

' "Press on, press on, looking forward to death! But it won't give you what you hope—only a deeper darkness still, the darkness of extinction." Who wrote that: a rebellious philosopher, someone driven to desperation by the horrors of the modern world, a drug addict on a suicidal trip?' (Guy Gaucher).

No, Thérèse of Lisieux wrote it, in bed, on 9 June 1897, three months before she died. She added: 'I shan't write any more or I might begin blaspheming. I fear I may have said too much already.' Yes, with Thérèse of Lisieux, you can expect all sorts of surprises. If the genius of her charity helps us to rediscover the grandeur of ordinary life and the dimensions of that true collective to which we all belong, her message contains another answer too—probably the finest present that she can offer us today, the one in fact that we need most of all. It has a name. For Thérèse of Lisieux it was the fruit of a struggle to the death with death. She insisted that it should be spoken of as part of her 'message'. Dearly she paid the price for the right to talk of it.

It is the finest of the fruits of charity. It was the ultimate gift left us by Christ, forsaken by men and facing death, as turning his Holy Face towards his Father and his brothers, he, crucified for us, cried out: 'My God, my God, why have you forsaken me?' Yes, that same cry, that same message, that same gift is offered us by Thérèse: the gift of hope against hope or, as she called it, her little way of trust.

But beware, her choice of words may give the wrong impression: 'little way', 'little soul', 'littleness'. Such turns of phrase could easily be misleading, were we to suppose they referred to something easy. For it means the ultimate acceptance of our life, and this is neither easy nor difficult. It isn't difficult but within everyone's scope, even when life seems much worse than one could ever imagine. It isn't easy, it's intoxicating: trusting through the darkness to the last drags everything into the void—consenting to follow Christ, to say 'Yes' to the last, since we are sure of being loved. And if, paradoxically, everything was so disposed as to throw Thérèse back on herself, whereas we have seen her outgoing in charity to the vastest collective that ever could be, so the same is true here: everything in her life seemed set to reduce her to despair, yet the reverse occurred: she discovered and rediscovered the way of hope.

The stars of day

When I consider this aspect of Thérèse of Lisieux's 'message', it always brings to mind a wonderful Russian legend called *The Stars of Day*. For it seems so well to describe her life and ours. Here it is: There are always stars in the sky but we cannot always see them, since the sunlight hides them. The stars of day, more billiantly beautiful even than those of night, can only be seen, says the legend, in deep, still wells. Perched high in the sky and invisible to the eye, these stars are only reflected in the bowels of the earth, on the black mirror of the water on which they shed their rays. And if we cannot see them when we look down from the wellhead, this is either because the water isn't dark enough, or because the surface of the water isn't still enough, or because the well itself isn't deep enough. Perhaps we shouldn't even be looking down the well from outside, but from the bottom of the well ... upwards.

You understand the drift of the parable? Our hearts one day amputated by sorrow, our lives at certain moments plunged in darkness and night, can be and are, in the world today, among our fellow-men, the wells in which the day-star is reflected, where it dwells—that loveliest of all stars, called Hope. This star is invisible to normal sight, it is without apparent existence, yet it can become visible when our lives reach rock-bottom. And then we are, as Thérèse also was, at one with the very heart of mankind. Yes, in the depths of distress, of defeat, of anguish, there shines hope.

Classic yet new: hope

By rediscovering the way of mercy, Thérèse challenges us to take a new look at God, and she also summons us to take a new look at man. 'Hope' is in fashion with theologians again. Yet note that the concept of Christian life as a journey, a pilgrimage, an exodus, is an absolutely classic one. St Paul defines a Christian by *'epectasis'*, that is to say, as a 'being-tending-towards-what-is-yet-to-come'. This concept was taken up and restated in one way or another by almost all the masters of the spiritual life. Gregory of Nyssa gives one of the earliest and most striking treatments of this in his commentary on Exodus where he portrays the Christian life in terms of the exodus of the Chosen People. Dionysius the Areopagite, St Benedict, Guillaume de St Thierry all try to pinpoint the stages or degrees of this itinerary; likewise St Teresa of Avila with her *Way of Perfection* and *The Interior Castle*, and St John of the Cross with *The Ascent of Mount Carmel*. Christian life is a journey, a crossing-over, something dynamic. But a number of novelties appear in Thérèse's message.

1. She does not talk about 'degrees of perfection', unlike previous masters of the spiritual life. She does not lay out her way as an itinerary with various stages. Faced with the details worked up into intellectual systems by the masters, experience shows her that she cannot follow these 'stages'. Her intuitions are thoroughly grounded in experience. It might be put like this: it's a simplification but gets to the heart of the matter; faced with the final stage, Thérèse is tempted to think, 'I am almost there'; but faced with the first one, she knows, 'I shall never get there'. It is this very impossibility of reaching the first stage which opens the way for her. Without beating about the bush, she adopts a much simpler, more colloquial synonym for the word 'way' (*voie*), to wit 'path' (*chemin*), when speaking of self-abandonment as 'the only path leading to that Divine Furnace', i.e. love, 'the only possession that I covet'.

2. Her way takes account of the most ineluctable facts of modern life and, one might say, those transitional situations inseparable from anyone's life (at this point theology and anthropology join hands):
—the point of departure of all life: desire;
—the point of breakdown: despair.
And she had experienced both to the full:
 Desire: to begin with, everything is object, object of a desire carried in her case to the extremes of anxiety. She is more or less forced to cultivate desire, partly due to the atmosphere of her home. Being the youngest, there was the business of trying to do as well as her sisters. (It is most important for a true understanding of the exemplary quality of hope in St Thérèse, as also for understanding the 'little way', not to juggle away the part played by desire: it is everywhere

at the outset, and persists to the end despite all set-backs, as *The Story of a Soul* bears witness.)

Despair: here we only need to recall Thérèse's way of the cross: her mother died when she was four; her sister and mother-substitute left for the Carmel when Thérèse was nine; the bewildering struggle with herself, lasting for three years and verging on neurasthenia, until her thirteenth year and Christmas conversion; her struggle to enter Carmel, in the course of which she tried every possible means and was still refused; her admittance to the Carmel, followed three months later by the trauma of her father's illness tormenting her almost to insanity. Then nine years of conventual life, distracted by her father's sufferings; next, the test, the ordeal of the final eighteen months: the trial of faith in a battle against despair, with the most absolute temptations to doubt about the future, about heaven, about God; and finally six months of agony and choking, culminating in the temptation to do away with herself. On the last day of all, her sister Mother Agnes was to throw herself at the feet of the Sacred Heart to beg that Thérèse, now at the very limit of her strength, might not fall into final despair.

It was as though God had allowed Thérèse's message to be authenticated before the eyes of the entire world; she was to live and push the possibilities of hope to their utmost limits.

The little way

Thérèse starts out from a double certainty (as we all do).

1.   First of all she discovers that within her she has an ineradicable and intense desire to love and to do good.

2.   At the same time, however, she realises that she will not even manage to climb the first step of the stairway which she would have to ascend to become someone worth-while, as she supposes God wishes her to be. 'I have always found, when comparing myself to the saints, that there is the same difference between them and me as between a mountain with its peak piercing the heavens and the obscure grain of sand trodden underfoot by people in the street.' 'The saints have also done silly things, but they did great things because they were eagles. Jesus, I am too little to do great things.'

3. Next, she encounters temptations, the same ones as ours. Revolt: other people don't understand; discouragement: all these brave desires will come to nothing; or pride and aggressiveness: I shall get there all the same, they'll soon see. And all this, cloaked in perfectly acceptable reasons: to do as well as her sisters, to become someone worth-while. As has been said, Thérèse competes in the world's holiness championship.

4. She then makes a decisive discovery: 'Instead of getting discouraged, I said to myself, "God wouldn't inspire me with desires which can't be fulfilled, so in spite of my littleness I shall aspire to holiness." ' If then, despite set-backs and temptations, that same indwelling desire resists and holds firm, this must mean (she reasons) that it isn't something of her own, but comes from God. And therefore her desire can't not be fulfilled, but by the same token it also means that the ideal, the picture that she has of herself isn't hers either. And thus she begins to learn to refer the picture she has of herself to someone else. But this is only a beginning.

5. And once more the set-backs, the incapacity, the helplessness grow worse, and this in connexion with what she very legitimately holds dearest: her family and her vocation. There is the tragedy of her father, there are the reverses suffered by her sister, Mother Agnes, when elected prioress of the Carmel; the reverses suffered by her other sister Céline during her first few years after entering the Carmel; and her own, too, as mistress of the novices; finally, the ultimate bewilderment of the trial of faith.

Here it is no longer a question of knowing that she is incapable of accomplishing what she once dreamed for herself, but of simply holding on as well as she can, in the darkness, day after day. An experience, be it said, shared by many, many people: over their work, over the future, over their children, over the problems of married life, over loneliness, other people's forgetfulness, ingratitude, hardship or pain. What many, many other people try desperately to do—to hold on and at the same time go on loving sweetly, trustfully—Thérèse did for years on end. 'The darkness seems to mock me, saying: You dream of light, you dream of possessing your Creator forever, you believe you will emerge from the encompassing fog. Press on, press on!. . . the darkness of extinction.' And she went on: 'I think I must have made more acts of faith in the last year than in the whole of the rest of my life.'

6. Then, the last discovery of all. She really has nothing left to rely on. Her strength? She has none left. Her desires? They have come to nothing. Other people's esteem, family pride? Her father's illness, nursed in a madhouse, a pitiful object at the last, had removed all illusions on that score.

What was there left for her to hold on to and still go on? Her little way. 'I am only a helpless, feeble child, yet my very weakness makes me bold to offer myself as victim to your love, O Jesus!' That is to say, only her weakness, her incapacity, her distress, her darkness, her nothingness as the means of reaching God and of forcing, by trust, the very darkness to have a meaning. Only from the bottom of the well, you see, will the day-stars shed their light. Whence Thérèse's shout of victory: 'O luminous Lighthouse of love, I have found the secret of capturing your flame!' That is the solution to the impossibilities which our ambition to love encounters: God himself puts 'his consuming flame' into our hearts.

Thus Thérèse grasps the decisive way in which hope reverses the situation: being a Christian doesn't primarily mean 'being someone worth-while'. On the contrary, it means learning, on account of our incapacity, to commit ourselves to someone else, learning to shift our fulcrum, since at this point we offer to God the one thing that he cannot get without us: the offering of our freedom. These were no pious thoughts where she was concerned. With heart, with blood, with life, she said: 'Mother, it's very easy to write edifying things about suffering, but writing conveys nothing, nothing! You have to be suffering to know!' And on another occasion: 'I am a baby and can endure no more!' One day when she felt seriously impelled to do away with herself and was on the brink of despair, she said: 'Perhaps I shall lose my reason. Oh, if you only knew how weak I feel!' Or again: 'A poor little nothingness, nothing more. . . .' And again: 'Alas, I am nothing but very weakness.' And again: 'For my part, the only insight I have is into my own little nothingness. And this does more for me than new insights on the Faith.'

Fr A. Patfoort observes: 'What all little souls must do—and we all belong to this category once we become aware of ambitions to love—is be able more or less at will to channel the invasive force of God's own love into the human heart. This is the secret. We have to realise how to take advantage of our littleness and transform it into a reason for trusting, and transpose it into the actual practice of 'bold' self-abandonment. We have to take God by the heart.'

The moment of truth

'To have passionately desired the All, to have kept herself from sin, to have sacrificed her entire youth by shutting herself up in a cloister and devoting her life to self-sacrifice, only to emerge into the darkness of extinction! Who could endure such a journey?' (E. Renault). That was Thérèse's moment of truth, the moment when she had to think everything out all over again. 'God now shows me the truth.' And again: 'Alas, I am back where I was to begin with! But I tell myself this with great contentment, not with sadness. How sweet it is to feel so weak and little!'

She had discovered the true face of the God of Jesus, offering himself to us in weakness and, like a beggar, waiting for our trust. And she knew that the time for total trust had come. Never to achieve anything worth-while again, but only to accept being exceeded—forever—by the excess of love confronting her. Then for her, as for the Good Thief, as for St Peter, as for the Samaritan woman, as for all the poor and sinful, the impossible step became possible: trust, making what in the end seemed too far away suddenly within reach. Exactly like the day-stars: but this is only revealed at the bottom of the well.

Adopting this attitude, that is, of accepting suffering—without bitterness—of consenting to be ground down by incapacity, by weariness, by helplessness, by sin itself perhaps: this itself becomes the way to poverty, and poverty obtains all from God. At a stroke, Thérèse exploded the grim threats which had been stifling Christianity for centuries and weighing us down for ages past. For generations of Christians believed that you had to become a hero, someone worth-while, to learn to have no feelings, to become like the gods as conceived by the Stoic philosophers of antiquity. You had to be worth-while to get near to God. Thérèse proclaimed the opposite: her little way, available to everyone, from desire to despair (which is the general human lot) can become for everyone, from darkness to trust, the road leading to God. Thérèse shows us that the way seemingly reserved for privileged souls, for great mystics, is available for everyone: yes, your anguish, your fear, your temptation, your weariness, can become the road to God.

And here she is one with the poorest, the most deprived and lost among us: with those who no longer have anything to rely on. And also one with the greatest revolutionaries, the great rebels: with those who do not wish to have anything to rely on beyond themselves.

For the rebel, God is dead, and so there is no one left to converse with. The rebel is autonomous at last, hence no more fear, no more limits. With the revolutionaries, Thérèse has very truly grasped the fact that within us we have an infinitely explosive force, that of the stars of day, much greater than any sun. But at this point their ways diverge. For her, our chance, our only chance ultimately lies in the foolishness of a God who is love and who has loved and still does love us to the point of folly, to the folly of lowering himself and becoming a beggar, to beg for our trust. 'All you who have wept or sinned, come and you will find strength and peace.' On one condition: that you do not seek any other strength elsewhere; and the decisive sign that we have found this infinite strength—of which rebels dream—is that we come to accept, yes to love and offer our very incapacity and weakness.

The extraordinary song of hope contained in the records documenting Thérèse's last ten months on earth may well be summed up in the words she gasped three months before she died: 'No, I'm not dying; I'm about to enter life.'

'My personal foolishness is to keep hoping. . .'

What Thérèse experienced (this purification and enlightenment by hope) is a providential prefigurement of what Christians surely need to experience today. Thérèse is certainly the saint for the twenty-first century. When the Church, like Thérèse in her own life, is collectively and individually undergoing trials, doubts, darkness at once excruciating and marvellous, for us Christians this must surely be the moment for trusting, the moment of truth. 'My personal foolishness is to keep hoping,' she used to say. What other foolishness do people expect of us Christians now? Yes, whether believers or not, we and our brothers can rediscover the brightest of day-stars, hope.

Here we owe it to ourselves to re-read what is certainly one of the high watermarks of spiritual and theological literature: I mean, the exchange of letters between Thérèse and her sister Marie of the Sacred Heart, dated 14, 16 and 17 September, 1896. 'If you had understood the story about my little bird, you wouldn't have asked me this. My desires for martyrdom mean nothing, they aren't what give me the limitless sense of trust which I feel in my heart. . . So how can you say, after this, that my desires are the sign of my love? I know for a certainty that this isn't what God finds pleasing in my little soul. What pleases him is seeing me love my littleness and my poverty; is the blind hope which I have in his mercy. You must try and understand this. The very desire to be a victim is enough, but you have to consent always to staying poor and strengthless, and that is the difficult part. If I could only make you understand what I feel! Trust, and nothing but trust, is what should lead us to Love.' This was written just a year before her death.

Mother Agnes was telling her one day how sad and discouraged she felt after committing a fault. Thérèse said, 'You don't do as I do. When I've committed a fault which makes me feel sad, I know of course that the sadness is the effect of being unfaithful. But you don't think I stop at that, do you? Oh, no, I'm not so silly! I make a point of quickly telling God: "My God, I know I deserve to feel sad, but let me offer it up all the same." ' 'I have nothing to rely on, no works of mine to trust in. So I could easily have decided to give up. But poverty has been a real light to me—a real grace. I realised that never in my life had I been able to discharge a single one of my debts to God, but that this could be my true riches and strength, if I wished it to be so. So I said this prayer: "O my God, I beg you, discharge the debt yourself." '

'Oh, if I were ever unfaithful, if I were to commit the very least infidelity, I think I should have to pay with terrible torments and that I could no longer feel resigned to dying.'—'What sort of infidelity do you mean?'—'A proud thought willingly entertained. If, for instance, I were to think, "I have acquired such-and-such a virtue. I'm sure of being able to practise it." For then I should be relying on my own strength, and when you do that you are in danger in falling into the abyss. What should I do, what would become of me, if I were to rely on my own strength! I understand exactly why St Peter fell. Poor St Peter was relying on himself, instead of on God's strength alone. I'm sure that if St Peter had humbly said to Jesus, "Please grant me the strength to follow you to death," he would have received it immediately. Jesus could of course have said to St Peter, "Ask me for the strength to do what you want to do." But no, because Jesus wanted him to understand how weak he was, and because he would have to govern the whole Church, which is full of sinners, Jesus let him experience for himself how little a man can do without God's help. Before St Peter's fall, our Lord said to him, "When you have recovered, strengthen your brothers." This meant: "Convince them by your own experience how feeble all human strength is." '

One evening while looking after her sister in the infirmary during matins, Mother Agnes asked her what she meant by 'staying a little child before God'. She replied, 'I mean, recognising one's nothingness, expecting everything from God, as a little child waits for everything his father gives him; I mean, not worrying about anything, not trying to get rich. Even among the poor, a child is given the necessities of life, but as soon as he's grown up, his father refuses to keep him any more and says, "You must go out to work. You can stand on your own feet now." To avoid having that said to me, I have made a point of not growing up. Being little also means not crediting oneself with the virtues one practices, under the impression that one is able to achieve something on one's own'; and five days before she died, 'The little will be judged with extreme mildness. And you can certainly stay little, even in a very responsible position, even if you live to be very old. If I had died at the age of eighty, if I had been to China or all over the world, I should, I am convinced, have died as little as I am today. And it is written that "at the last, the Lord will arise to save all the meek and humble on earth". It doesn't say to *judge* but to *save*.'

Digging desire deeper

By this approach, Thérèse of Lisieux admirably expresses the two aspects of Christian hope and the reversal which these involve. (Whether expressed in terms of classical or biblical theology, the essential thing about Christian hope is the same.)

In the first instance, hoping means waiting for happiness. We desire more than we can give ourselves ... some future, possible good, though too difficult to acquire on our own. I am condemned to desire the 'always more'. The tribulations of hope are the tribulations of desire, or more exactly of the idea which we create of ourselves through the projects and dreams which we weave and renew day by day.

The first law of hope is thus simply this long education of our desire, a much more exacting education than you might suppose: for we run up against reality and this teaches us to 'purge' ourselves: that is to say, to maintain and intensify our desire, the very nature of which is to increase; and at the same time to accept the limiting factors of reality (though relinquishing nothing of the violence of our desire for holiness, for happiness and ultimately of our desire for God). 'I have always wanted to be a saint. So I can, despite my littleness, aspire to holiness.' And again: 'Your love prevented me from childhood, it grew with me and now is an abyss the depths of which I cannot sound. Love attracts love and so, Jesus, my love leaps towards you, longing to fill the abyss attracting it.' And again: 'My desire might seem rash, when you think how weak and imperfect I was and still am. Yet I still feel the same bold confidence that I shall become a great saint.' And again: 'I am not an eagle, I simply have an eagle's eyes and heart. For in spite of my extreme littleness, I dare to gaze into the Divine Sun, the Sun of Love, and my heart harbours all the Eagle's aspirations.'

Promise or Covenant?

And so, with Thérèse as with the lives of all the saints, we necessarily come to a second aspect of hope. It isn't possible not to be aware of the gap between what we want and what in the long run we can procure on our own. And so we have *to appeal* to someone else to get what we desire. What we now hope for is no longer happiness, bliss itself, but the means of obtaining it: God's helping help (*Deus auxilians*) and this *at once*. Hoping now means not only possessing the end, but at the same time henceforth possessing the means of obtaining the end. In this case, God himself. Thus God is now not only our aim, our end, our 'omega point', bliss and so forth, but first of all our ally, aid, help, recourse.

In biblical terms, we might say that hope bears on two things:
1. *The promise*: God promises Abraham a posterity: 'Your reward will be great'; promises the Blessed Virgin a child, 'Your son will be the Son of the Most High';
2. *The covenant*: For the object of the promise to be obtained, God affirms his covenant with them: 'I shall be with you. I shall be your Suzerain.' 'Do not be afraid, the Lord is with you. The Spirit will cover you with his shadow.'

Thérèse very quickly grasps the concrete application of this: first, God-Bliss; and this presupposes doing the truth. And this is the first battle: digging desire deep. This is a fiercer battle than you might suppose, not a simple one at all, you have to get rid of all illusions. Secondly, God-Ally-Aid; your fulcrum has to be changed, you have to learn to trust. 'A philosopher said: "Give me a lever and fulcrum, and I shall lift the world." What Archimedes couldn't achieve, since his request was not addressed to God and since he had only physical effects in mind, has been obtained in all its fullness by the saints. As fulcrum, the Almighty gave them *himself* and *him alone*, and for lever he gave them prayer kindled by fire of love. And with these they did lift the world; and with these the saints of the Church Militant go on lifting it and saints to come will go on lifting it until the end of time.'

Thus, in putting forward her 'little way', Thérèse goes much further than what we take to be the end-point of the Gospel and of hope. We are inclined to think that we have got there once we realise that, being loved by God, we can interpret ordeals as 'purifications', ultimately beneficial, of the process of waiting; that hoping means having to wait longer than we expected. Thérèse goes further. She grasps and lives that essential Chrisitan reversal: of the two aspects of hope, what comes first is not, as we suppose, God-Happiness, God-Bliss, but God-help, God-Ally. The convenant has to come first and, if we are faithful to the convenant, then we discover the full extent of what God promises, the full extent of bliss. Provided that we fight the battle, and this consists in relying on someone outside ourselves, and not on out own resources. And the clear and practical sign that we have changed our fulcrum is that we now make it our joy to offer up our incapacity. This is where hope and prayer and our understanding of Christ, of his self-abasement, his '*kenosis*', and our understanding of mercy and the reciprocity of love which God wants to establish, all converge. In this lies the whole shift in St Thomas Aquinas's theology, as influenced by Alexander of Hales. Hope always has two objects: God, end and final cause; and God, help and efficient cause. And of these two aspects, the most important is God's help, for in asking for God's help, we cannot ask for less than God himself. 'Hence,' writes Fr Patfoort, 'Thérèse did not need to grow up before liberating her vast ambition to love and presenting it to the Father; and by this I know that my present misery arouses a sense of tenderness in him, making me a privileged soul, and that it only depends on me, with his grace, for me to benefit from this personalised tenderness.'

We see that, for Thérèse, the problem gradually ceases to be one of striving towards self-fulfilment according to a pattern achieved spiritually (we might say, according to 'integral nature') with the help of grace, degree by degree; but rather of enduring the excess of mercy to which God wishes to lead her. And this is what ultimately burns her up: this going-beyond-herself, to which he invites her. And this is the 'glory' to which she feels called: the rich diet of the Incarnation henceforth shared; not merely the grace to help her become a fully human personality, like some further form of medication, but the actual sharing in life divine. On 25 April 1897, Thérèse wrote to the Abbé Bellière: 'I feel as though I shall never be ready (for Heaven), if the Lord doesn't himself deign to transform me. He can do it in a second; after all the other graces he has lavished on me, I am still waiting for this from his infinite mercy.' And on 21 June, she added: 'I am the way which Jesus lays down for me. I try not to think about myself, and what Jesus deigns to work in my soul, I ✓ leave entirely to him.'

The way of the Good Thief

But this is more than she can manage; she realises that it is unendurable to be condemned to wait longer than you can go on giving yourself. And here, she offers her way; it might be called the way of the Good Thief, the way of freedom and hope, through weakness, incapacity and even sin, for we are half sinful, half obedient child, and she grasps that the sinner's experience and the child's experience are ultimately the same. For the child can endure to be outdone, since his very helplessness is all he has to offer. Then hope and expectation become the fairest fruit of love. There is nothing more precious that you can offer to God than this nothingness and this ✓ hope, since hope includes nothingness. Only love understands the law of love's increment. 'It hopes for all.' 'To have given' is the essential thing and will be so forever. The most precious thing we have to offer is hope itself; this is the fairest present that Christ has given us: hope against all hope. 'Why have you forsaken me?'

It might be objected—though that would be a caricature of what Thérèse meant: 'Isn't all this very easy? Works are of no value? God doesn't need us if all we have to do is offer up our defeat.' Beware, giving your nothingness involves a reversal, a total about-face.

To be able to give your incapacity, you have in a certain sense to have already given everything else. You have to give everything, ✓ layer by layer, down to the bone. And then you have to give what is most precious of all: your consent to be more and more blinded by God and to have the joy of no longer trying to understand for yourself. Faith wasn't Thérèse's problem, but this self-committal presupposing hope. And, once again, this is neither easy, nor difficult: consenting that Christ should love us. In this sense, the theology of 'glory' and that of the Good Thief are the same. There is this ultimate battle of free choice: the power to say 'No' and the absolute gravity of this 'Yes' or 'No'. The little way is the art, for all the 'little', of infallibly bringing about (their helplessness and sense of unworthiness notwithstanding) the realisation of their infinite ambition to love, by the simple fact of daring to count absolutely on God's fatherly love. In the ultimate analysis, Thérèse shows all those 'little people' who have no special mission, no talents, no spiritual euphoria, that the ambition to love and the certainty of being able to do so, far from being inaccessible, are offered to them on a preferential basis. And then, in a flash, we realise that there is no other Christian greatness outside this way. 'The weaker you are, with no desire or virtues, the more apt you are for the operations of this consuming and transforming Love.' For the poor are those to whom the Kingdom of Heaven belongs.

6

EVEN DEATH ...

By her understanding of charity, Thérèse of Lisieux gives us a new
view of life, of the 'greatness of the everyday'. As the prophet of what
the whole Church is now obliged to practise more and more: hope,
trust to the last in spite of the darkness, Thérèse gives us a new
outlook on defeat, weakness, anguish and distress. So now let us
consider how she allows us to recover what in life is most essentially
ours—what in existence is at once most inevitable and most unpre-
dictable; what is at once most precious and most tragic; what no one
else can experience in our place, yet what is being taken away from
us, being more and more efficiently stolen from us. This is perfectly
in order, in one way; we should be overwhelmed if we knew the date
in advance. But things were not always so. Today, as never before,
we fear it. And everyone is of a mind—doctors and family and those
we love; when the moment comes, public opinion and in the ultimate
analysis, deep down, *ourselves*, to do everything in our power to let it
happen without anyone's noticing. Suspecting that if it were given to
us to know when it would occur, to go through it all in advance, we
might lose control and run mad, we arrange things in such a way
that we avoid encountering it at all. This is a terrible thing; and
today we are robbed of it more and more efficiently. You already
know what I mean: our encounter with death.

'I have seen a saint die; it isn't as you'd expect'

To give a better idea of the way Thérèse can help us on this point, I
quote the testimony of three very different men, each testimony
being very forceful.

First, that of a very distinguished professor of history, H. I.
Marrou: 'By watching Thérèse living out her suffering—and, worse

than physical pain, the barbarities of useless medical treatment—
and her slow descent to death, modern man can glimpse what faith,
the true Christian faith, really is.'

The second testimony is from the writer Bernanos: 'I have seen a
saint die, and it isn't as you'd expect, it isn't like what you read in
books, I can tell you. You have to steel yourself to watch it. You see
the soul's armour cracking apart.'

The third testimony comes from one of Russia's greatest living
writers, A. Siniavsky, formerly a Marxist, later sentenced to a
labour-camp and now living in France. He writes: 'Of the world
religions, Christianity plays the part of the shock battalion, the punishment brigade thrown in where things are most dangerous, at the
hottest part of the front. Where the hand-to-hand fighting is thickest,
there the death-battalion is thrown in. They blow up their bridges
behind them. Look at them, the heroes of Christendom. You won't
find many prudent ones among them. Their story is a long succession of martyrdoms and deaths, undergone by a phalanx following
their God's example. They are soldiers, displaying their scars and
wounds to the world as decorations. And who enlists with them?
People of all nations, the scum of the earth, even criminals, but
always those who have taken the cross. Anyone can join: the ignor-
ant, the sinful—provided he is ready to throw himself into the battle.
It is the religion of maximum hope born of despair. Nowhere do you
find such close contact with death as in Christianity. Fear is not
absent. But it is transformed into a force able to pierce a breach in
the tomb and spurt out the other side. Not the contemplation of
eternity, but the possession of eternity, in battle, with one sole
weapon: the readiness to die.'

The Russian author's description fits Thérèse like a glove: the
readiness to die!

'There will always be time to suffer the opposite later'

'I have seen a saint die, and it isn't as you'd expect.' What was it like
for Thérèse of Lisieux? Let her speak for herself.

Was she preserved from fear and anxiety? No, she didn't know
how she would measure up. Several times during her last six
months, she was to say, 'I wonder how I shall measure up to dying. I
hope I shall acquit myself with honour! All the same, I suppose it
doesn't really depend on me.' On another occasion, she was even

less confident: 'How am I going to measure up to dying? I shall
never know how to do it!' Believing her to be firm and resolute at the
prospect of death, her companions attributed this to youthful illusion and told her that she would certainly be afraid, to which she
replied very simply, 'That may well be so . . . I never rely on what I
think myself, but I want to make the most of the thought which God
has put into my head for the moment. There will always be time to
suffer the opposite later.' There was nothing extravagant about her,
no illusion. The nuns thought she must have been receiving certain
consolations because she had started writing poems again. She then
said, 'You probably think that I am a soul filled with consolations,
for whom the veil of faith is wearing thin. But it isn't a veil now, it's a
wall reaching up to the skies. When I sing the bliss of heaven, the
eternal possession of God, I feel no joy in doing so. I am merely
singing what I want to believe.'

Her sisters and companions were later to testify to this
herculean—and childlike—battle, the ultimate test of the little way.
For eighteen months, 'in the tunnel, in the darkness', she underwent
the trial of faith. ' "If you only knew," she said to me, "the frightful
thoughts that plague me! Pray hard for me not to listen to the Devil
as he tries to make me believe his many lies. The arguments of the
worst rationalists fill my mind. Dear Mother, why must I have such
dreadful thoughts when I love God so much?" She went on to say
that she never argued with these dark thoughts. "I endure them of
necessity," she said, "but even while having them, never stop renew-
ing my acts of faith." '

Sister Marie of the Trinity was to state: 'Sister Thérèse of the
Child Jesus had to endure terrible temptations against faith. One
day when she was telling me about the darkness which she was
enduring, I said to her in amazement, "But what about those
radiant poems you write? They contradict what you have just been
saying!" She replied, "I sing of what I want to believe, but I do so
without feeling any of it. I won't even tell you how deep the darkness
is in my soul, in case of being instrumental in making you share my
temptations." ' And Sister Thérèse of St Augustine: 'She admitted
something to me which surprised me strangely. "If you only knew
the darkness into which I've been flung! I don't believe in eternal
life; I think, after this life there will be nothing more. Everything has
vanished for me." ' But she added afterwards—and this is the point,
'All I have left is love.'

Though in the punishment battalion, in the thick of the fight, she
doesn't turn tail, but neither does she strike attitudes, is neither

conceited nor complaining. And yet there is fear there, though she does not linger over that. Her secret is elsewhere; it comes from her absolute loyalty to Christ. To her sisters, she would repeatedly say, 'Don't be upset, dearest sisters, if I suffer a great deal and if you see no sign of happiness in me when I reach the point of death. Our Lord too died a victim of love, and see what his death agony was like!' She was to recur to this idea: being ready to die like a soldier of Christ is different from what you might expect. 'Our Lord died on the cross in agony, yet his was the finest of deaths for love. . . . The only example, indeed. Dying of love doesn't mean dying in transports of joy.' No transports of joy, no consolations, no ecstasies: she even had to give up receiving communion. And this was shattering for her, the very limit of what she could endure. This scandalised several members of the convent: imagine a Carmelite dying without the sacraments! Thérèse heard what was being said and this only added to her suffering. Six weeks earlier, she had said, 'Of course, it's a great grace to receive the sacraments, but when God doesn't allow me to do so, that's good too. *All is grace.*'

'All is grace.' Yes, but that doesn't prevent her from crying on 20 August, doubting survival after death, forsaken by the God whom she cannot receive, while the other nuns shake their heads over her. 'All is grace.' Thérèse lived that out to the last.

So here we have a young women of twenty-four. A year previously, on Good Friday, she had her first haemorrhage of the lungs. She quickly realised that the sign might prove to be fatal. Her health improved for a bit. But a year later, after Lent, the illness took complete control. On 30 July, she was not expected to last the night. Being robust however, she lingered until 30 September. The medications of the period were as follows. We quoted Professor Marrou a few pages back as referring to 'ineffectual barbarities'. But unfortunately these were the only remedies known: blistering—a cataplasm bound round the chest sometimes for hours at a time to raise enormous blisters, which were then burst in the hopes of relieving the lungs; cautery, sometimes on five hundred different spots at one sitting, and much else. Her sisters were terrified at seeing her undergo such treatment. Then, as well, the torments natural to sufferers from TB before modern times: that is, death by thirst and suffocation. And the side-effect of her illness: gangrene of the intestines. Next, the mental suspense of waiting day after day for death. They got ready for her funeral in July. Lastly, the spiritual torment of darkness and the night of faith.

Of this, the book of her *Last Conversations* allows us to follow her progress from day to day—a document unique in Christian history. If any member of my family had to face death today, this and the Gospels would be the only books I should recommend him.

'I am no more immune than anyone else'

What truthfulness, but also what strength!; the strength of weakness that puts its trust in, relies on, the One for whom it waits. And, as well as the sense of humour, the unheard-of gentleness and silent consideration for others, what joy! On some days, everything is transformed: 'It's not death coming to take me; it's God. Death is only a phantom, a nasty ghost like you see in pictures.' Again: 'Dearest sisters, oh, how happy I am! I can see that I'm soon going to die.' And one day, when the chaplain asked her if she were re-signed to death, she replied, 'Father, the only resignation I need is to staying alive. Joy is what I feel at the thought of dying.' But this didn't stop her being ready for anything, whether joy or fear. 'Why should I be more immune to fear of death than anyone else? I don't say, like St Peter, "I shall never deny you." ' She becomes impatient to die: 'I don't rely on the illness. That leads me there all too slowly. All I count on now is love.' But there were still another three months to go before the day. Two months later she said, 'Now that God has done what he wanted to do, he will come like a thief at a time when we least expect; that's what I think.' And a week before her death, when someone said, 'Oh, what a terrible illness! How you must have suffered!' She replied, 'Yes! what a mercy it is to have faith! If I didn't have faith, I should have killed myself without a moment's hesitation.'

And now

What can be said about this battle, this herculean race, behind these simple, commonplace externals? She had of course encountered death already: her mother's death, her father's death; and going into the convent was also a kind of death in respect of everything that she left behind. But the battle between faith and death is something different, something deeper and more personal. Thérèse's first con-clusion was this. She grasped the fact that death is not merely some-thing waiting for us *later*, something only occurring at the end of our lives. No, throughout our days we live in a state, the temporal state, in which all is fragile, friable, fleeting, where things and people pass away. 'Every moment is a passing away, every moment of our lives is a dying.' Here she is at one with today's most eminent philosophers when they define man as a 'being-made-for-death', that is to say, as the only animal able continuously to site things in their mutability against an immutable horizon. So Thérèse's conclusin is simple: if everything is passing away, there is only one reality which counts, what I actually have in hand, by which for the time being I escape death's clutches: the present moment. It is sacred, because it comes from God. None of it must be wasted, since it permits me forthwith to reach the end and, because of this, to do little things as well as big things, and thus to conquer death.

There is also a second conclusion: in our existence, death is the one inevitable event, one which has to be undergone, against which we are at our most defenceless. And that is why, as we have already said, we do everything we possibly can to conceal it. We don't die any more, we fade out. We hide death as though it were today's unique obscenity. We chase it away, refuse to acknowledge its existence. Not least, we Christians are accomplices to the universal vanishing-trick. By the same token however, bereft of death, our lives are in danger of losing their tension, of feebly trickling away, of becoming a sustained deception. But are we to go along with this supreme perversion, with this supreme collapse? Thérèse proves that we can do more than just put up with death; we can transform it into a free, awaited act, taken in our stride, transfigured by trust and faith. We can make it into an offering. We can all make an offering of the very thing that crushes us.

This doesn't stop us being afraid of it or of having to endure its onslaughts like everyone else. Thérèse of Lisieux reminds us that fear and anquish can be transfigured by love and hope, and that each of us can rely on an inner force strong enough to overcome the inevitable. Are we to go on depriving ourselves of the only thing that can change the meaning of our death: *the opportunity of offering it with Christ*, the opportunity of associating ourselves with him in his Passion? If we give in on this point and go on suppressing our awareness of death, one day (it seems to me) there will be nothing, no difference whatever, to choose between having faith and not having faith. For my part, I don't want to die without knowing. I know I shan't put up much of a show, when possibly laid low and racked with anguish, but with all my strength I pray I may be able to offer it with Christ and not have it stolen away from me.

Bernanos grasped the point very clearly in *Lettre aux Anglais* ' "Oh, Mother, is this the end?" little St Thérèse of Lisieux asked the Prioress in her death agony. "How am I to behave as I die?" Probably Joan of Arc had the same thought on the morning of 30 May, 1429. What delights us in these childlike words is not that they defy death, but that they welcome death with a kind of discreet timidity, spoken as though in fear of giving death offence. By this we recognise the perfection of a sort of heroism, to serve and bear witness to which—we realise to greater or lesser degree—is what life demands of us. Suppose the words are in themselves childish! Childish words like these raise up men.'

'I am entering life'

There is one matter we must raise, concerning ourselves in the Church of today. By wanting to return to 'earthly realities', by wanting to strive for 'the promotion of human values' (which is certainly urgent and necessary), don't we run the risk of thinking of everything from a purely earthbound point of view? And don't we ultimately run the risk of limiting our horizon to the earth itself? And by eliminating the ideas of preparing for death and what comes afterwards, by not mentioning them, by not wanting to think about them any more, isn't there a foreseeable risk that we, yes, we Christians, will make death even more frightening and horrible than it is?

Here Thérèse of Lisieux reminds us of that last victory of faith over all fear, in the name of the reality of 'heaven' already begun and henceforth already possessed. 'I don't see how I can have more after my death than I already have on earth. I shall see God, that's true, but as far as being with him is concerned, I am that completely already, here on earth.' Yes, everything has already begun. 'How sad life is!' one of the nuns was moaning to her. Thérèse replied, and says the same to us, 'Life's not sad. Exile is what's sad.' 'I am not dying, I'm entering life.'

7

MERCY: 'A POLLUTED IDEA'?

In one of his sermons, St Augustine marvels that the Good Thief
should have had a better understanding of the Bible than the doctors
of the Law. And he begins questioning the Good Thief to find out
whether he has been studying the Scriptures between his acts of
brigandage; how has he succeeded in understanding Isaiah 53, when
the doctors of the Law couldn't see that it was being fulfilled before
their very eyes on Calvary and thanks to their own machinations?
Why had the Good Thief chosen to confess his faith in Jesus at the
very moment when the disciples had given up believing in him? And
St Augustine puts this simple answer into the Good Thief's mouth:
'No, I haven't studied the Scriptures, but Jesus looked at me and in
that look I understood everything.' Which we might put in another
way and say: unless in a sense you have understood everything
without having to have it explained, you understand nothing about
Christianity.

'Jesus looked at me and in that look I understood everything.'
What Thérèse understood, she summed up in one word. A word
repeated at each of the big moments of her life. An inexhaustible
word. In the days of Jesus, it was totally novel, incomprehensible
and explosive, though it has become devalued and worn out since. It
is, it comprehends not ideals but the very life, the very heart of God.
Those who live their lives in partnership with Christ have wept to
experience it. Today we neutralise it, and yet it contains the one
reality which, today as never before, can help us go to the limits of
ourselves to plumb God's ultimate secret. This supreme reality,
made available to us once more by Thérése of Lisieux, is mercy.

She begins her life-story by saying, 'I am only going to do one
thing: start singing now what I must repeat for ever: the Mercies of
the Lord.' She ends the story by saying, 'How will the story end? I
do not know, but what I do know is that the Mercy of God will
accompany it for ever.' And what was the climax of her life to be? An

act of self-offering to Merciful Love: 'May my soul fling itself without delay into the everlasting furnace of your Merciful Love.' Later having found her true way, 'this vocation of love,' how does she explain it to her elder sister as she begs her to try and understand it? 'My desire for martyrdom is unimportant. What pleases him is the blind hope I have in his mercy. This is my only treasure.' It's clear: her only treasure. 'To me he has given his infinite mercy, and through it I can contemplate and adore the other divine perfections! I see them all as radiant with love, even Justice seems clothed in love. So what should I fear?' The last sentence of Thérèse's last letter reads: 'He is love and mercy—that is all!' In the Church's heart, henceforth and forever more, the message of Lisieux is that of mercy; for Thérèse gave her life so that we could have a better understanding of what that means. Mother Agnes, her sister, was under no delusion about this. When asked at the Process of 1910 why she wished to see her sister beatified, she gave this one spontaneous answer: 'Because it will procure the glory of God, principally by proclaiming his mercy.'

Salvation or liberation?

But are we really sure that we understand what mercy is, lying as it does at the heart of the Gospel and revealing that new face of God, and for which Christ chose to die? Haven't we worn its meaning out and lost our taste for it? The debates over 'salvation and liberation' surely prove the point. People even go so far as to talk of a 'polluted idea' which ought to be removed from the Christian vocabulary forthwith. . .

This repudiation of the notion of mercy isn't anything new. At the time of Christ it was so explosive that everyone rejected it. For each of the categories or sects claiming possession of the truth, the idea of being led by faith to receive, to accept salvation in the name of their very wretchedness and poverty was intolerable. Alike for the Essenes—monks who had withdrawn into the wilderness and for whom flight and separation from the world, including even the rejection of marriage, could alone assure a purity worthy of God. Alike for the Zealots—freedom-fighters and guerrillas for whom political struggle and revolution against the occupying power could alone assure the re-establishing of the temporal messianic kingdom, which (they held) was the real objective of the divine covenant. Alike for the Pharisees—who were the apostles of popular religion, of adaptation to the dictates of circumstance and hence of the evolution of a code of prescriptions which, if obeyed, would give man the means of working his own salvation. But whether they fled, or rebelled or propounded a reach-me-down salvation, none of them felt any further need for mercy or for God.

Thérèse has left on record how much she would have liked to learn Hebrew, so as to understand the Gospel better. And this no doubt would have been a great joy to her. For few Hebrew words are etymologically more rewarding than those used to convey the concept 'mercy'. Four words are used to convey the reality: *hanan*, to lean over; *hamalnoum*, to suffer with, to spare since one feels pity; *raham-rahamin*, to be soft, the mother's breast, the entrails, the womb; and *naham*, to relieve someone, stop his groans by helping him to breathe. What a programme! Thérèse saw this as God's, with regard to man.

Under sentence of death

In trying to go beyond the commonplace externals and grasp the true quality of Thérèse's intuitions on this subject (on a par, be it said, with those of St Augustine, Thomas Aquinas, Pascal, Luther and other geniuses who have puzzled over this mystery and its problems), we should remember that the meaning of mercy is by no means self-evident. And we can classify the difficulties as coming in part from ourselves and in part from the Gospel.

From ourselves? Why, of course we have ideas about justice and mercy. Very early in life, we become aware of other people. We know what it means to feel ill or to do wrong, and by the same token we ought to know what 'mercy' is: 'A heart that takes on another's misery'; 'a heart taking others' misery to itself, because it loves'. But—and sometimes it takes us a whole lifetime to realise—when we want to relieve misery, we hardly ever do it in the name of mercy, but nearly always in that of compassion or of justice. Now the sight of misery is of course abhorrent to us; so, since we do not ourselves want to suffer, we do our best to relieve it, our motive being compassion; or we revolt and make a fight for it. And this is fine. Or again, we have possessions while our neighbour is in want and distress, we feel the injustices of the situation and take action, we give, we fight; but here we are motivated by justice and in the last resort we are often more concerned about liberating ourselves than about loving our neighbour.

'Living the misery of others', as Christ did, taking our place with the condemned, among the condemned, as an innocent who has deliberately got himself arrested so as never again to be in a position to pass judgement on others: this is far beyond justice or compassion. To live out our neighbour's misery as though it were our own, since we cannot rid ourselves of loving, this being God's unique law. For us men, this experience is beyond us. Christ and his look alone can make us understand that such a thing is possible.

But there is also another difficulty, and this comes from the Gospel itself. There we encounter two faces of God: the face of infinite yet immediate love, but also the face of justice. A rigorous, stern God whom we encounter in many passages, in the Sermon on the Mount for instance. 'Make haste and put your affairs in order while you are still on the way. You will not get out of there,' our Lord tells his disciples, 'until you have paid the last penny' (Mt 5:26). And, as opposed to this, the God of infinite kindness who seems completely blind in the way he washes away the past for the woman who had been a notorious sinner, for Zacchaeus, for the woman of Samaria, for Peter who had betrayed him, for the Good Thief.

So what are we to do? Which face are we to follow? To escape the dilemma, we evade it, we make a compromise. We attenuate justice and mercy by means of each other and in a flash empty both of their reality. We think, 'God is just, but that's not very important since he is good and, we are told, he is love.' At the same time, we add, 'God is merciful, but let's take care and not rely on that too much, since he is also just.' Millions of people have suffered over this dilemma. Which is the measure by which our lives will be weighed? The Church and mankind with her have been tormented by this for centuries. Where is the true face of God?

'The humiliated Face'

Thérèse realises that the question is all-embracing and that it requires an all-embracing answer. To the abyss apprehended as awaiting the deliberate choice of evil or of breach with God, her intuition postulates another abyss: that of mercy.

Here surely is the most remarkable expression of her very vigorous and intelligently realistic faith. The two abysses are connected: as she sees it, God doesn't choose 'beforehand', not 'without' her freedom of choice, not without being aware of her incapacity. As she sees it, true knowledge of God is achieved rather by adopting certain practical attitudes than by affirming theoretic principles. It can never be said often enough that, since the Incarnation, practical problems are what bring us most effectually face to face with the truth about God. Since the Incarnation took place in history, so each individual's salvation will take place in history. Thérèse was extremely clear-sighted about the truth or duplicity of our practical attitudes. And the problems in question are often agonising. 'My temptation is despair,' said the Curé d'Ars.

We must not forget the dramatic conditions in which Thérèse like an explorer, was to re-open the breach, to open her way, her 'little way', her way of trusting in mercy.

1. To the crushing weight of anguish inevitably felt by anyone at the thought of his faults and the future was added, in her case, the suffering caused by a faulty presentation of God. The Jansenist tone of much of her approved reading is enough to make you shudder, particularly the *Theological and Spiritual Lectures on God's Greatness* by a seventeenth century Capuchin, whose admirable patristic learning inspired his pen to incredible lengths in his treatment of love, as also of terror. Mother Agnes found it terrifying; not so Thérèse.

2. Also it happened in the midst of a family drama, concerning the being she loved most of all—her father, kept in confinement, supposed to be insane, locked up in a madhouse—that Thérèse two years after entering the Carmel, in 1890 read this page in the fifty-third chapter of Isaiah and in it discovered the ultimate secret of mercy: the veiled face, the humiliated face of the condemned innocent, Christ. The two pictures coalesced in her mind: Christ and her father. He was then in the Good Saviour Hospital at Caen, a madhouse with three thousand inmates. She remembered—though still without understanding its full meaning—her premonitory vision at Les Buissonets, where her father's face had appeared to her, covered with an apron. He had a habit of covering his face with a handkerchief when one of his attacks came on. Humiliation and anxiety seized on her at her most sensitive spot, provoked on the one hand by other people's remarks: 'How are the mad folk today?' . . . 'So they've taken him to Good Saviour's, have they?', and on the other, by the nagging thought in her own mind that he had fallen sick because she had taken the veil. For her, mercy was no mere concept.

She bore the misery of another, of precisely him whom she loved most of all.

Thérèse bore her father's illness and wasn't content merely to 'endure' it by passive acceptance, as her sisters courageously did. She 'loved' this ordeal and through it discovered 'the humiliated Face'.

Faced with the pain, illness and dissolution of others, Thérèse saw primarily, not justice, but mercy. Later, when she had reached the depths of her own misery, she saw, not her father's face, but God's face veiled in its turn. Herself eaten away by disease, she pushed her certainty of mercy to the limits. This was how the 'little way' was tested—by illness, the night of faith, and death.

'You want justice?'

We can sum up this certainty of hers by two stories.

1. 'I cannot fear Purgatory', she would often say, trying to communicate her own confidence to her sisters, though never succeeding in doing so. And to Sister Febronie who was arguing the case for divine justice, Thérèse then said (and here we have surely one of the simplest yet most inspired answers to the problem in Christian history): 'Sister,' Thérèse said, 'if you want divine justice, you will get divine justice. The soul gets exactly what it expects of God.'

Such in a nutshell is the Christian answer, absolutely sure, absolutely theological, absolutely simple, absolutely evangelical, summing up the whole thing: 'We are the ones who decide, we are the ones who make the choice.' An answer both thoroughly reassuring and very alarming.

Reassuring since it all depends on us; the choice is ours. God leaves it to us.

2. But it is very alarming too, and here Thérèse takes us one step further. For in fact her answer implies a rider. Obviously we all imagine ourselves ready to choose mercy, we are all 'for it'. But choosing mercy isn't quite what we suppose. We are in favour of mercy in so far as it suits our book. We are always ready to exploit its benefits and take advantage of it. When it seems to suit our purpose, we think we are choosing it, when all in fact we are doing is trying to

Knowledge of God without that of our misery equals pride.

Knowledge of our misery without that of God equals despair.

Knowledge of Jesus Christ strikes the balance, since in him we find both God and our misery.

PASCAL

Who would believe what we have reported? And to whom has the arm of Yahweh been revealed?

> He had neither beauty nor honour; a man of sorrows, he was despised, someone from whom people avert their eyes; he was despised. Yet it was our diseases he was bearing, ours the pains that he was carrying. For our rebellions, he was wounded, the punishment reconciling us fell on him, and we have been healed by his bruises.

We had all gone astray like sheep. For our rebellions, he was struck dead. For offering his life, he will see his descendants.

> Since he bore the sin of many, since he interceded for the rebellious, I shall give him a multitude in reward and a mighty victor's portion will be his.

ISAIAH 53

make use of it. Thérèse detected the misunderstanding: God's mercy is sweet, without a doubt, and much sweeter than we imagine, but it doesn't fit into our scheme in the way we think. These are the final words she wrote in her little exercise-book, in an exhausted hand, the last few lines in pencil, to warn us, 'Yes, I'm sure, even if I had every sin that can be committed on my conscience, I should go, my heart broken with repentance, and throw myself into Jesus's arms, for I know how much he loves the prodigal child who returns to him. It's not because God in his prevenient mercy has preserved my soul from mortal sin that I raise myself to him in trust and love.'

No, the benefits which she had received were not what gave her confidence. Thérèse had quite rightly seen the fearful paradox, that same which had so perplexed Luther, *viz.* that if you do not love mercy for its own sake, you will not 'choose' it! If you do not want it independently of the benefits which you hope from it, you find yourself unable to choose it, even for the sake of being saved—for you are still demanding justice. You would like to be able to get away with it without having to love, without having to lay down your arms, without needing to approve of, or consenting to concur in such total dependence on God's love.

After making her self-offering to Merciful Love in 1895, Thérèse was often to come back to this topic. To another nun, Marie of the Trinity, who relates, 'I was extremely frightened of God's judgement, and in spite of everything that Thérèse could say to me, nothing made this fear go away', Thérèse replied, 'There is only one way to force God not to judge us at all, and that is to appear before him empty-handed.' 'What do you mean?' asked the nun. 'It's very simple,' Thérèse replied. 'Make no reservations, give whatever you get as soon as you get it.' 'But,' objected the nun, 'if God doesn't judge our good actions, he will certainly judge our bad ones, and what about that?' 'Do you understand what you're saying?' Thérèse replied. 'Our Lord is very justice; if he doesn't judge our good actions, he will not judge our bad ones. For those who offer themselves to love, I don't think there will be a judgement at all; on the contrary, God will make haste to reward his own love which he will see in their hearts. We are only consumed by love in so far as we abandon ourselves to love.'

'For those who offer themselves to love, I don't think there will be a judgement at all.' Cynics will possibly be tempted to take these words as mere religiosity, suitable for the professionally devout. But to my mind they mark a very peak of Christian thought: and the only answer to everyman's ultimate agony, whether he is a believer or not, when faced with his own inadequacies, his weakness and the problem of evil. Someone else had already said exactly the same thing, although we tend to forget this: 'Whoever believes in him will escape judgement' (Jn 3:18). Was Thérèse saying anything different? 'For those who offer themselves to love, I don't think there will be a judgement at all.' We are saved and, as of now, 'we escape judgement' because we believe spontaneously in God's promises, because we love them in themselves, because we are in affinity with them, because we are caught, magnetised by the source of these very promises—which is love, mercy. No longer are we concerned with exploiting it or of making use of it to derive benefit from it; it demands to be adopted, to be loved for itself as the whole point of living, as we love a face, that ultimate face: God. That is the heart of this attitude and this saves of itself, as Scripture tells us, being trust, being faith in him who loves us, trust to the last.

And if faith, if trust saves us, this doesn't mean that we are therefore dispensed from being good (as Luther was tempted to think), but that it cannot but bring a deeper goodness to birth in us, a goodness deeper than ourselves: a goodness consisting in awareness of God's own tenderness, since we are already caught by, bathed in, baptised into, invested with, this tenderness, this grace.

'If we fall, yet persevere in love to the point when the soul can no longer repress the cry, My God, why have you forsaken me?, if we stay at this point and still go on loving, we end up reaching something which is no longer unhappiness and is not joy, but is the central essence, essential, pure, not sensible, common to joy and suffering—the very love of God' (Simone Weil).

8

'JUSTICE, MY LAD, ISN'T YOUR CONCERN'

The Norwegians have a saying: 'Fish rots from the head down.' And
the same applies as regards the head, the essential thing, for the
Christian: the instinct of mercy. It can easily make everything else
go bad, if it isn't in good health and working order. Sometimes it
goes hard or develops an excessive rigour, puritanism, stoicism, purity or fury against the wicked; sometimes it degenerates into
indulgence, complaisance, understandingness, 'broad-mindedness'.
All motives are acceptable: be they political necessity, maintenance
of tradition, defence of institutions, the need to 'arrange things',
'pluralism' now so indispensable, and so forth. 'Where are the
philosophers now? What no eye has seen and no ear has heard,
things beyond the mind of man. . . . The depths of God can only be
known by the Spirit of God . . .' (Cor 1:18—2:16).

So where did Thérèse acquire this extraordinary, all-commanding
instinct:

and her love of God,

and her right understanding of the Church as regards its misery
and grandeur,

and her refusal to give way to despair, her courage to struggle
against evil,

and her missionary vocation,

and, dare we say it, her 'political' dimension for our world
today?

The facts speak for themselves; it is up to us to draw our conclu-
sions.

The murderer of the century

In the summer calm of the little household at Les Buissonets, on 1
September, 1887, Thérèse anxiously opened the newspaper, *La*

Croix, and in it found one of the decisive signs of her life:

The vile blackguard who murdered the three victims of the Rue Montaigne was executed this morning, and with him ends the disgraceful scandal of the past few days. The Place de la Roquette and the adjoining streets were crowded from an early hour in the morning. At 11.30 p.m., mounted and foot detachments of the Republican Guard and departmental police took up their position in the square. There were a few shouts of 'Long live Boulanger!' in the Rue de la Roquette, but all the other streets had been sealed off. At 2.55, two waggons arrived bringing the materials for the execution, and these were assembled by the light of hurricane lamps.

At 3 a.m. precisely, the venerable Abbé Faure drove up in cab no. 3751, which was harnessed to a white horse. He was followed shortly afterwards by M. Athalin, the examining magistrate, M.Taylor, the chief of police, M. Garon, his second-in-command and M. Martigny, the secretary. At 4.45, M. Bauquesne, the prison governor, M. Baron, the commissioner of police, his secretary and the Abbé Faure made their first visit to Cell 2, then occupied by the condemned man.

Pranzini was sound asleep. M. Bauquesne had to shake him twice to wake him. Marie Regnault's murderer sat up, gazed distractedly about him and uttered a hoarse shout. What an awakening! For the fact is, the wretch had all along been convinced that he would be pardoned. He made wild efforts to stammer out a few words. 'You're about to commit a crime. I'm innocent!' And making a violent effort to appear calm, he added, 'The only thing I regret is not having been able to kiss my mother.' He then suddenly became deathly pale. 'Pull yourself together, Pranzini,' said M. Bauquesne. 'Your crime is too serious for the President of the Republic to grant you a pardon. Die like a man and thus make amends for your crime.' 'I'm innocent! I'm innocent!' he shouted. The two detectives handed him his socks. He put them on slowly, while the clerk read him the sentence. Trembling, he put on his clothes, babbling incoherently. He then asked for some cold water to wash his face and hands. M. Faure, the chaplain, then spent a few moments alone with him. Pranzini said to him, 'I shall be as calm as you are, for I die an innocent man.' He was then taken into the registrar's office, where Deibler (the executioner) and his assistants were waiting for him to be handed over to them. There they cut his hair, widened the neck of his shirt and pinioned his arms. At two minutes to five, while the birds were singing in the trees of the square, a confused murmur swept through the crowd, the command, 'Draw your sabres!' rang out, the clatter of metal was heard, blades flashed, the door of the prison swung open and there on the threshold, pale as death, stood the murderer. The chaplain took position in front of him to spare him from seeing the fatal engine. The executioner's assistants held him to right and left. He pushed the priest and assistants aside. Once at the guillotine, Deibler gave him a push, throwing him forward. One of the assistants standing on the other side of the guillotine grabbed his head, positioned it under the lunette and held it steady by the hair.

But before all this could happen, a glimmer of repentance may perhaps have crossed his conscience. He asked the chaplain for his crucifix. He kissed it twice. And, the blade having fallen and one of the assistants having seized the severed head by its ear, we may wonder whether, human justice being satisfied, this last kiss may not have satisfied divine justice too—whose primary requirement is repentance.

These were the very words that Thérèse read that day. She was then fourteen. In 1895, eight years later, Thérèse still remembered them and made this episode into one of the crucial moments of her life when writing her autobiography.

'My first child'

'I heard of a great criminal who had just been sentenced to death for horrible crimes. The circumstances made it seem likely that he would die impenitent. I wished at all costs to prevent him from going to hell, and to do this I used every means I could think of.' So Thérèse must have heard people talking about the murderer. From that moment, she was actually to make herself responsible for him. Because Pranzini had been sentenced to death and was going to be executed and showed no sign of being sorry for what he had done, she set about doing everything within her power to save his soul. And from that date onwards, she studied *La Croix* for any 'sign' of the prisoner's conversion.

Eventually, on 1 September, she discovered the article quoted above. 'Pranzini had not made his confession, he had mounted the scaffold and was about to put his head through the fatal hole, when suddenly, seized by a lightning inspiration, he turned round, snatched the crucifix out of the priest's hands and three times kissed its sacred wounds!' Thérèse comments: 'I had obtained the sign I asked for, and that sign faithfully reproduced the graces which Jesus had granted me, to encourage me to pray for sinners. Hadn't the thirst for souls entered my heart while contemplating the wounds of Jesus and watching his divine blood flowing from them? I wanted to give sinners that immaculate blood to drink, so as to purify them of their stains. And the lips of "my first child" were to fasten themselves on those sacred wounds!!! What an ineffably sweet reply!'

For Thérèse this decided her vocation. The sign was to direct her towards Carmel. 'Ah, after that unique grace, my desire to save souls grew stronnger every day. I seemed to hear Jesus saying to me, as to the woman of Samaria, "Give me something to drink!" '

On 20 March, 1887, at 17 Rue Montaigne, [now the Avenue Matignon] in Paris, was discovered the lifeless body of Régine de Montille, with those of Annette Grémeret her maid, and of a little girl of twelve called Marie [Régine's daughter in fact, though passed off as being her maid's] All three had had their throats cut in the most brutal manner, and the mistress's jewels had disappeared. Madame Régine de Montille was really called Marie Regnaud. A beauty, she had been seduced when very young and then deserted in the capital. There she had caught the eye of the Comte de Montille. She was to be seen at all social gatherings, where Parisian society was doing all it could to forget the horrors of 1870 and the Commune. This notwithstanding, a high-spirited, good-natured girl and devoted to her child. . . . The triple crime made an enormous sensation, as much on account of the personality of the victim as of the conditions in which it had been perpetrated. All the daily papers described the triple murder of the Rue Montaigne with a wealth of horrid detail, thus ensuring unprecedented sales. And, admittedly, every ingredient was there to titillate the public: a sinner of great personal beauty, a maid faithful to death, and little Marie Grémeret the sacrificial lamb, not to mention the guilty man himself, a veritable monster of monsters. (G. Gaucher, 'Thérèse Martin et l'affaire Pranzini', *Vie Thérèsienne*, no.48).

Fascinated and terrified:
'You might have thought you were at the theatre'

When the police brought Pranzini back to Paris from Marseilles, it was decided not to let him get out at the Gare de Lyon since there was a crowd waiting for him—though not to lynch him. It was largely made up of women—a first sign of an exclusively feminine infatuation which was later to make this executioner of women into a legend. Getting out at Charenton, Pranzini entered Paris in a convoy of five cabs. His trial opened in a court-room packed so full that even people with special tickets of admission signed by the presiding judge, M. Onfroy de Bréville, could not get in. The latter had been beseiged by hordes of society ladies, and the appearance of the court-room was most unseemly. You might have thought you were at the theatre or, to be more precise, in the Presidential Enclosure at the races, since the summer's day (Saturday, 9 July) was radiantly sunny, calling for little white veils, parasols and fans. There were even feminine hands to focus lorgnettes in the prisoner's direction. The presiding judge got angry and had to order the society women to stop their chattering. Maitre Demange—Pranzini's defence counsel—spoke to such effect that he drew applause from the people present in the court-room. Noisy demonstrations and shouts of 'Quash the case! Quash the case!' marked Pranzini's transfer to Grande-Roquette prison. His photograph was on sale on the boulevards, so were broadsheets telling his story. Of all the many letters addressed to him, often accompanied by chocolates or cigarettes, the only ones he was allowed to receive were those from his mother. And once the President of the Republic refused him a pardon, a veritable riot broke out round the walls of Grande-Roquette. At nightfall, on a word given by no one knows whom, the fashionable world united *en masse* to advance on the prison. A long queue of carriages along the Boulevard Voltaire disgorged women dressed to the nines and men in top-hats, and these marched forward alongside men in cloth caps and bareheaded girls. Such singleness of purpose had never been seen; it suggested the very passing of a social order. And this composite crowd, squeezing into the square where the execution was scheduled to take place, shouted for Pranzini's pardon' (Ibid).

'I felt ashamed of being so excited'

I don't think anyone can honestly pretend not to be secretly fascinated, terrified, even intoxicated, at the sight of evil. The same Parisian mob as shouted for Pranzini's case to be quashed was to roar for Buffet and Bontems to be executed. You may not remember the case but in 1972, crazed with despair, the two men barricaded themselves in the prison hospital at Clairvaux, taking a nurse and warder as hostages—both of whom had families to support—and later cut their throats. R. Badinter, counsel for the defence, wrote:

I could tell that they had reached the law-courts. A long shout of 'Death sentence! Death sentence!' had risen in the street as the black marias—looking very much like paupers' hearses—came along. This was what people had been waiting for, much as the bull is awaited in the arena. But it wasn't impatience or the happy-go-lucky excitement of a race-meeting that gripped the public now. Fear and hate were weaving an invisible net round the still empty dock. As I ostensibly concentrated on sorting out the papers in my file, I was thinking that this, as far as the defence was concerned, was the worst threat of all, and far more sinister than the facts themselves or the arguments of the prosecution. The crowd demanded one thing, and what it demanded was the death sentence. This was what I had to fight against.

My colleagues joined me, the judge took his place: 'Guards, bring in the accused!' An immense sigh filled the court-room. So there they were—the Clairvaux murderers!

The trial was everywhere. Posted up on the news-stands, reported on the radio, the subject of every conversation. I went out into the street. I could feel its presence in everyone I met. I felt ashamed of being so excited. I went into the first cafe I came to. At the counter, the trial—or rather the pointlessness of the trial—was the only topic of conversation. In forceful tones, with accompanying gesture, a customer was saying, to the approval of all listening: 'Creatures like that, they ought to be put down—quick sharp—as simple as that. And this is how!' And down came the blade of his hand on the counter. I remembered how a colonel in the Parachute Regiment had summed up his conception of justice in three adjectives: 'Justice, to my way of thinking, should be implacable, immediate, summary. That's what people want. Everything else is mere twaddle.' I could see that the colonel had plenty of disciples at Troyes. Though the colonel for his part had struck lucky. A system owing nothing to popular justice had sentenced him in all due form to life imprisonment for his part in the last round of plots against the government. He was now amnestied and a free man. I sometimes wonder whether this rigorous spirit regretted not having his theory of justice applied to himself. Or if he was now prepared to concede that the cautious approach and solemnities of justice had something to be said for them after all.

The head-warder was waiting for me in the office. 'Well, how did you find him?' he asked. He then went on, as though to himself, 'If only he would sleep at night. You know, he never stops smoking, one cigarette after another. It's the same with Buffet too. He walks up and down his cell. He never stops all night.' I listened. He for one felt no hate for the Clairvaux murderers. So everything was possible, I thought, if they were pardoned. I said good-bye to the head-warder. To my surprise, he thanked me for coming, much as a relative in hospital might thank the doctor. We shook hands. I was glad for Bontems' sake that he had this warder in charge of him. By this time, Bontems wasn't a man like other men. He was already somewhere else from the rest of us, in a sort of marginal zone inaccessible to the living, though not yet actually death. As I went out into the prison-yard, I noticed that it had started to rain.

'Was there anyone?'

As never before, I had seen the face of hate laid bare. And hate had carried the day. I knew what hate looked like. People of my generation have often had occasion to see it. But hate takes on the worst face of all when assuming the mask of justice. Rabid hatred is terrifying, but judicial hatred is shaming. I remembered the upraised fists, the grimaces of the crowd surrounding a shaven-headed girl as two armed men proudly dragged her half-naked through the streets for having made love with the Boche. Hate however always confers an unexpected dignity even on the worst of criminals. You forget the guilty man, you only see the hunted creature, the victim of disaster. Mauriac describes a young villain who had killed an old woman to rob her. When the crime was being reconstructed, he was escorted through a crowd of people by the police. Struck, insulted, spat on, his face became Christ's face. Those who are carried away by hatred do not realise what a gift they confer on the very object of their hatred.

But hatred makes you question everything, not least the kind of justice that hatred applauds. The uproar, the applause greeting Buffet's and Bontems' death sentence was still ringing in my ears. The presiding judge might well use his gavel. The hunt was over. The beasts had been captured. And no doubt the crowd would also have applauded if the executioner had held up the brace of heads for them. Yet in days gone by, when Gilles de Rais, the arch-criminal of all time, was on his way to the stake, as he went by, people all fell on their knees begging God to have mercy on the sinner's soul. Buffet was no Gilles de Rais—far from it. Was there anyone, who did not know him, to implore God's forgiveness for this murderer whose only wish was to die? I should like to think so. I hope so. But I never met him in the crowd thronging round the law-courts.

Nothing could alter the fact that we had encountered hatred and been carried away by it.

We have all to some degree had our part in the trial of the Clair-vaux murderers. If I have quoted the testimony of Bontems' defence counsel (Bontems had been sentenced to death for complicity, although he had not killed anyone himself), I do it for two reasons.

I know of no other testimony better able to evoke Thérèse's own encounter with justice, prayer and mercy as she experienced it in the course of Pranzini's case, and make it intelligible to us at the present day.

But also because, in the present day, Thérèse was also present in the tragedy of these murderers. Bontems had a photograph of Thérèse in his cell. To the cry of Buffet's counsel, 'Was there anyone to implore God's forgiveness for this murderer whose only wish was to die?' an answer has since been given: the Carmel at Lisieux was praying with Bontems, and Buffet knew it.

The image of the Crucified

You could hardly put it better than Guy Gaucher does in comment-ing on Thérèse and the Pranzini case:

In this tragedy, everything might, you would think, have repelled her: brutal murders, sexual excesses of victim and murderer, cupidity, the sordid context (if she knew all these details). At the time, no one spoke of anything but 'the vile blackguard', 'the monster', 'the ignoble brute'. Yet for her, he was 'the poor, unfortunate Pranzini' and she adopted him as her 'first child'! The force attracting her to him had nothing in common with the sick emo-tions of the women who blew kisses to the notorious seducer. She went towards him in evangelical simplicity of heart.

The image of the Crucified had revealed Thérèse's missionary vocation to her, and the encounter with Pranzini occurred immediately afterwards.

She was not drawn to the criminal as a reaction against her own sur-roundings but exclusively by Christ's saving love which she had just discovered. Pranzini was the living experience of this. But of course this does not preclude the fact that grace was acting on a physical being. Thérèse was then in full physical and spiritual efflorescence. Her femininity was certainly a factor in her being attracted to Pranzini at the moment when her vocation of spiritual motherhood had been indelibly imprinted in her. We may add that Thérèse was never to forget her 'child', even though his name was never to occur again in her writings for the rest of her life. This particular secret she shared only with Céline. In the convent, she went on having masses said for Pranzini. Céline testified to this at the Process: 'The Servant of God used to call Pranzini "her child". Later, in the convent, whenever she was given any money for her birthday, she used to obtain permission from our Mother Prioress to use it for having a mass said, and she told me on the quiet, "This is for my child; after all the tricks he got up to, I should think he needs it! I mustn't forsake him now." ' Then, as earlier (in 1887), she was afraid 'she might be obliged to admit that the masses being said' were for Pranzini.

Marcel Moré makes an excellent comment on this statement of Céline's: 'Such a jocular way of referring to someone who had killed three people! Clearly, this was Thérèse's method of hiding a secret lying very near her heart. The memory of the murderer seems never to have left her. But then, how could any woman forget her first-born, especially having borne him by the light of grace? It is all too obvious that from the year 1887 when Pranzini's 'crime' occurred, to the year 1897 when on her deathbed she suddenly uttered the word 'crime' in her sister's presence—Celine must have been completely astonished—she had faithfully preserved Pranzini's picture in the depths of her heart. When she exclaimed, 'If I had committed every crime imaginable . . .' she was breaking a silence lasting for ten years and only interrupted by the writing of her autobiography. Every crime imaginable! There can be no doubt that in a general sense she meant all the crimes of mankind, but it is no less certain that more specifically she was referring to the ones committed by Pranzini.'

Yes, Pranzini did play an important part in Thérèse's life, long after 1887. The murderer of the century, who like the Good Thief had been able to enjoy the benefits of Mercy, had put the youthful Thérèse on the track of the essential truth: that felons and whores are summoned to believe boldly in Merciful Love, since Jesus did not come to call the righteous, but sinners. In an environment, where a murderer was no more than a monster ripe for the guillotine, a child rediscovered the spirit of the Gospel.

Can we save souls?

On Thérèse's missionary vocation, Guy Gaucher writes:

It was been said and repeated all too often that Thérèse lived in a closed environment, sealed off from the hubbub and problems of the world. Consequently we tend to think of the saint of Lisieux as not being of her age, as

existing outside time. Once again the holy picture prevails over reality.
Suffice it here to list a few topics for further research:

—Thérèse and Pranzini, which subject is by no means exhausted, despite
Marcel Moré's excellent work.

—Thérèse and Hyacinthe Loyson, the ex-Carmelite friar and former
preacher at Notre-Dame, Paris, who got married, founded his own church
and was frequently in the news. Thérèse never stopped praying for him and
offered her last communion on his behalf.

—Thérèse and Henry Chéron: as a child she had met, in Guérin's the
chemist's where he was working, a man who was later to become mayor,
member of parliament and minister, a notorious anti-clerical, leader of the
'materialists' against whom her uncle Guérin strove and for whom Thérèse
prayed and offered her life.

—Thérèse and Leo Taxil: the imposter of the century, a writer of anti-
clerical pamphlets, who hoodwinked Catholic opinion by a false conversion
before unmasking himself on 19 April, 1897. Thérèse had written to Diana
Vaughan, a supposed convert invented by Taxil. In pursuance of the fraud,
Diana replied to Thérèse's letter.

Was she really insensitive to the problems of her times? Investigation of
these four topics alone would show the passionate interest she took in contemporary questions, in those at least concerning the deeper part of man. By
loving intuition, the saint of Lisieux had grasped that Jesus spent his life
among sinners to save them. She did not enter Carmel to escape from them,
to insulate herself from contact with them, but by burying herself in silence,
prayer and the martyrdom of love for their sake, to take her place at table
with them and with them share the bread of affliction.

Thérèse constantly uses the word 'atonement', showing us in
practical terms what the true import of this doctrine is. If this doctrine is true, it is a very grave and in certain respects sinful matter for
people to minimise it, not only people leading the consecrated life
but also Christians at large. For if it is true, it follows that, for lack of
atonement, men are in danger of not being saved.

The doctrine of atonement is such an essential part of Christianity
that without it there wouldn't be anything left, since our salvation
entire is the fruit of an act of atonement: Christ's atonement. 'They
were our diseases he was bearing, ours the pains that he was carrying ... For our rebellions he was wounded, he was crushed for our
transgressions. The punishment reconciling us fell on him, and we
have been healed by his bruises' (Is.53:4-5). 'He has overridden the
Law and cancelled every record of the debt we had to pay; he has
done away with it by nailing it to the cross' (Col. 2:14).

By inviting us to the banquet of divine life and by virtue of that
same love which nailed him to the cross, God summons us (in order
to give us even more) to share in this atonement, by making up in

our own bodies what is lacking to the Passion of his Son. We may feel ill-equipped at such a prospect, but this means that we still don't really understand it, since God is offering it to us only to give us even more, not to demand more of us. He wished and wishes 'to save sinners by means of sinners', in such a way that sinners share all the privileges of innocence, including this one. The doctrine of atonement affirms that he who is saved is not separate from the Saviour but, on the contrary, that the process of being saved involves an invitation to become a saviour too. In Christianity, we do not save by building on the fruits of the Redemption but by sharing in the Redemption itself, i.e. in the repairing of a ruptured love. Whatever may be said, there is a debt to be paid, but far from being inconsistent with love, the necessity actually springs from love itself. What repairs love and reconciles what has been ruptured is sorrow shared over the wrong done, are tears shed over this very rupture.

Next to Christ, who could claim to have been more afflicted by evil than the Virgin Mary? Yet wasn't she preserved absolutely from all sin?

If we aspire to anything more than insubstantial dialogue with God, we have no choice but to consider, to some degree at least, what this in fact involves: God leaves us free to choose to be separated from him. God has been ready to give us a divine privilege, his own prerogative: the absolute power of choice, though with the attendant risk that we may choose to be our own gods. Hence, be it said, 'in heaven' God's eternal gratitude will be on those who have consented to live this privilege out in union with God and who, having renounced living to themselves alone by exploiting this power in which we resemble him, have built their liberty out of love for God's love.

In practical terms, this means that by discovering that we have a positive power for good and for saving others and that, with Christ, we are involved in the Redemption (which alone can harness all our powers to the full), we find a living 'solution' to our anguish. We do not 'see', but we are sure of performing actions of eternal efficacity. The consequence of refusing remains a secret with God: the Church may canonise but has never damned anyone. We need once and for all to grasp that we have nothing less than God as our hope. All the same, it must be quite obvious that the theory of the non-existence of hell tends, like an anaemia, to void the cross of Christ of all significance. Even if unversed in theology, those seized by love of God know this to be so.

Having discovered the problems involved in our vocation and in our freedom of choice and how these can go wrong, we then have to learn to approach God, no longer in innocence and despite these setbacks, but precisely as sinners and relying on our very distress, that is, on his mercy.

What God then shows us is that he is love at a depth that we had never suspected, the evidence of which comes as a comprehensive answer to all the difficulties of Christian life. And then only does brotherly charity assume its truly mystical dimension, that is, its rigorously Christian one.

We only learn pity through the wounds we suffer. 'After the Resurrection,' writes Pascal, 'Jesus wished to be touched only on his wounds.' Thérèse's pity and wounds didn't need to come from sin. Her clear-sightedness, her awareness of her frailty, the harshness of her life, were enough. Her father's humiliation, her illness, her setbacks, her impulses, her struggle . . .

From all of which she distilled three attitudes:

—towards God, an absolute and bold assurance;

—towards her community and her 'brothers', an ever-renewed understanding;

—towards herself, a refusal to feel disgust.

1.   The bold lover

Unthinkable at this point not to quote the parable of the two children and the clever doctor. Once again, under commonplace externals, Thérèse speaks with prophetic genius. No page in the tradition of Christian spirituality explains more succinctly how we can grasp what mercy is when we find ourselves to be the recipient of it: here we are on the very threshold of the mystery of the Immaculate Conception—our Lady more sensitive to evil than any other creature because preserved from evil by mercy. And Thérèse was bold enough to bracket herself with Augustine and Mary Magdalen . . .

'Yes, I am well aware, Jesus knew that I was too weak to be exposed to temptation. I should probably have let myself be burnt to nothing by its deceptive light if I had seen it glittering before me . . . It didn't fall out that way. Where stronger souls meet joy and then out of loyalty renounce it, all I meet is bitterness. I claim no merit for not having succumbed to love of creatures, since I have only been preserved from this by God's great mercy! I can see that without him

I might have fallen as low as Mary Magdalen, and our Lord's profound words to Simon echo very sweetly in my soul. I know this to be true: "He who is forgiven less, loves less." But I also know that Jesus has forgiven me more that he forgave Mary Magdalen, because he has forgiven me in advance, preventing me from sinning. How I wish I could put into words what I feel!'

'Here is an example which to some extent expresses what I think. Imagine the son of a clever doctor. He trips over a stone, falls down and breaks a limb. His father hurries to him, lovingly picks him up, tends his injuries using all the resources of his art and soon, completely cured, the son shows his gratitude. Now, this child certainly has good reason to love his father! But now let us consider another case. The father, well aware that there is a stone lying in his son's path, hurries ahead and, without anyone's seeing, takes the stone away. Now obviously, this son, the object of his prevenient love, not knowing what a misfortune his father has saved him from, will not show him any gratitude and will love him less than if he had been cured by him. But if he then gets to know about the danger from which he has just escaped, won't he then love him more? You see, I am that child, the object of a Father's prevenient love, he having sent his Son to redeem, not the righteous, but sinners. He wants me to love him because he has forgiven me, not much, but ALL. He hasn't waited for me to love him as much as Mary Magdalen did, but wanted me to know how he loved me with an ineffably prevenient love, so that I shall now love him to the point of madness!'

'I don't make for the first place but the last. Instead of stepping forward with the Pharisee, I confidently repeat the prayer of the publican. But more than all else, I copy the behaviour of the Magdalen; her astounding or rather her loving audacity which charmed Jesus' heart seduces mine. Yes, I am sure, even if I had every sin that can be committed on my conscience, I should go, my heart broken with repentance, and throw myself into Jesus's arms, for I know how much he loves the prodigal child who returns to him. It's not because God in his prevenient mercy has preserved my soul from mortal sin that I raise myself to him to trust and love.'

'She would say to me: "Does a father scold his child when the latter admits he has done wrong? Does he inflict a penance on him? No, of course not; he presses him to his heart."'

'To illustrate this thought, she reminded me of a story which we had read in our childhood: about a king who was out hunting and gave chase to a white rabbit. His hounds were just about to catch it when the little rabbit, realising that all was lost, turned swiftly about and jumped into the hunter's arms. The king was so touched by this demonstration of trust that he insisted on keeping the rabbit ever after and wouldn't let anyone else handle or feed it except himself. "And this is how God will behave to us," she said, "if, pursued by justice, symbolised by the hounds, we seek refuge in the very arms of our Judge." '

'I don't understand, dear brother, how you can doubt you would go straight to heaven, were the infidels to take your life. I know you have to be very pure to appear before the God of all holiness, but I also know that the Lord is infinitely just; and this justice, so alarming to many, is the very reason for my joy and trust. Being just doesn't only mean being severe in punishing the guilty; it also means recognising good intentions and rewarding virtue. I hope as much in God's justice as I do in his mercy. Because he is just is why "he is compassionate and very tender, slow to punish and abounding in mercy; for he knows our weakness, he remembers that we are but dust. As a father feels tenderness for his children, so the Lord has compassion on us!" (Ps. 103:8, 14, 13). Dear brother, as we listen to the Royal Prophet's words, how can we doubt but that God can open the gates of his kingdom to his children who have loved him to the point of sacrificing everything for his sake, who have not only left family and country in order to make him known and loved, but who are even willing to give their lives for the One they love . . . Jesus was certainly right in saying there is no greater love than this (Jn 15:13)! How could he let himself be outdone in generosity?

'That, dear brother, is what I think about God's justice; my way is all trust and love, and I do not understand souls who are afraid of such a loving Friend. When I read this or that spiritual treatise, in which perfection is represented as being hedged about with a thousand obstacles and encompassed by a host of illusions, my poor little spirit soon grows weary; I close the learned book, since it only puzzles my brain and dries up my heart, and I turn to Holy Scripture instead. Then all appears clear, a single word opens a vast horizon to my soul, and perfection seems easy; I see it is enough for me to recognise my nothingness and abandon myself like a child into God's arms. To great souls, to great intellects, I leave those fine books which I cannot understand, far less put into practice, and take delight in being little, since only children and those who are like children will be admitted to the heavenly banquet (Mt 19:14; Mk 10:14; Lk 17:16). I am very glad that there are many mansions in God's kingdom (Jn 14:2), for if there were only one—the description of and means of access to which are both beyond my wits to understand—I should not be able to get in.'

A 'bold lover' ... the quotations available are endless, and the matter is so important that we shall return to it in Chapter 9.

2. Understanding and mercy

Try the experiment of talking about mercy in the Church. Take as your concrete examples, for instance, the remarriage of divorcees, or priests who have left the ministry—you can be sure of being criticised, snubbed or even denounced. This is to be expected. It is impossible to put this choosing of mercy into words, precisely because it is a concrete choice. For us to know whether we have really and truly chosen mercy, Christ has given us one clear and effective sign: 'Blessed are the merciful, for they will receive mercy.' This perhaps is the deepest point from which all Christian 'commitment' should begin, starting with political commitment: the hatred of evil because evil is intolerable. There is no need to go over all this again. The facts quoted in Chapters 3 and 4 above speak for themselves.

3. Beyond disgust

There is another sign proving that we have allowed mercy to enter our lives. It is equally trustworthy. I do not mean as concerns God and his unconditioned generosity, but as concerns ourselves and our own nauseous natures. I mean, a certain attitude to life, to our hopes, to our failures.

There is in fact a paradox in the Gospel. To be his disciples, Christ summons not the indulgent, the soft or the complacent, but warriors. 'If anyone loves his father or his mother more than me, he is unworthy of me.' And each of the Beatitudes is a summons to battle. And this seems difficult, impossible to us. And so we recoil in fear.

But this is because we hear these summonses, we receive them, as our hearts—our still-too-hard hearts—interpret them to us. They alarm us all the while we have not made the choice and opted for mercy come what may. What we actually hear is: 'He who wants to be my disciple must carry his cross proudly, must carry his cross

tirelessly, must carry his cross courageously, perfectly. . .' And this
is just not possible. But to follow the God of Mercy is something
quite different. What is meant is not that we must take heart because
we shall be courageous and victorious thanks to our own efforts, not
at all. It means understanding those other calls of Christ: 'If you are
tired and weary, come to me; if you are meek and humble of heart, if
you become like children again, then you will be my disciples. I
came for the lost sheep, I did not come to call the righteous.' So he
who aspires to be my disciple must certainly carry his cross. But he
will be saved by fear, if he knows, if he admits that he is carrying it
'deplorably', as best he can, tottering along, very often dragging
behind. 'We must weakly carry our cross', Thérèse remarked. Yes, if
we love mercy, we must consent to leading our lives and carrying our
cross deplorably badly. Only then do we know that we haven't been
cheating, we know that we've reached the light at the last. Yes, says
God, this is all I ask of you, and you will be my disciple.

'I felt like being sick,'—'No, even that, even your nausea, lay that
on me as you may. It won't be anything to be proud of, but you will
already know what mercy is, and then you will know who I am and
who you really are.'

An advocate, Jesus Christ the righteous

How many times Thérèse must have experienced those truths enun-
ciated by St John!—'We have an advocate with the Father, Jesus
Christ the righteous' (1 Jn 2:1), and 'If your heart condemns you,
God is greater than your heart' (1 Jn 3:20).

Let us go back to Robert Badinter's testimony for a moment,
where he interrupts his account of the Clairvaux trial to let his
former master speak about the barrister's profession.

'Justice, my lad, isn't your concern. You don't have to mete out justice, you
don't decide anything, you don't pass sentence on anyone, you can't even
acquit anyone. Your problem isn't to know what is just or unjust. Your only
problem, your only reason for existing as a lawyer, is to conduct the defence.
Understand this, my lad, it's perfectly simple. Don't think: "What I'm
doing I'm doing for the sake of justice." Sometimes this may be true, sometimes not, but in any case it isn't important. What counts is that you're
doing your best for the defence. Defence, my lad, is indivisible. By which I
mean that you must give your whole self to it. Defending isn't something to
be done in a detached way. Defending means never yielding an inch of

ground, never letting the prosecution rest on its assumptions, even means refusing to accept hard fact. For the defence lawyer there can only be one hard fact. And that is that no one is ever guilty.'

Jesus didn't forgive in the abstract. The only person in a position to forgive the torturer is the person being tortured. Only someone who has been the object of hatred and its thirst for destruction can demonstrate the impotence of hatred by forgiving the hater, in the hopes that this action will be the beginning of a new life for the person then under hatred's sway. The forgiveness which Jesus gave at the moment of dying: "Father, forgive them", was a forgiveness pregnant with his whole life-story. He had been hunted, denigrated, beaten up, despised, ridiculed, sentenced to death and now was dying like any criminal and blasphemer. By forgiving, Jesus hoped that the logic of death, to which he had himself fallen victim, would not have the last word. His forgiveness opened the possibility of a future, and this future is thenceforth inscribed in the fact of his resurrection. God has made Christ's forgiveness his.

Jesus opens the future to the sinner, since he testifies by his forgiveness that no one is once and for all shut up in hatred, and that his God is the very One who throws down all barriers by forgiving those who murder his Ambassador. By this act, forgiveness is acquired for every man, since he who pronounced it is forever alive. No longer may God be called on to maintain the mutual hatred of clan, of race, of class. He cannot even be invoked now as the guarantor of an implacable justice. God can only be invoked where forgiveness creates a new relationship. By liberating us from hatred by his forgiveness, Jesus liberates us from the oppressive image of the Absolute.

'All are called'

In 1945, Bernanos asked Malraux what he considered was the most important event of our times. Malraux replied, 'The return of Satan', Bernanos on another occasion remarked that being a Christian didn't merely consist in believing in God—which was easy—but in believing in the Devil too.

We might take this a step further. What does *not* believing in the Devil mean? In the last resort, surely, refusing to choose mercy. . .

By rediscovering the face of the true God, the God of Jesus, Thérèse became a missionary to the whole world. She rescues us from that worst of maladies. She brings us the ultimate remedy for evil. And this is summed up in three words: 'All are called.' If evil exists, no evil can exist, for her, before God, beyond the reach of mercy. Good and evil do not exist in parallel: as though evil might in the last analysis be beyond God's power.

It is a terrible malady, whatever its origin: starting with what originates in Christianity itself (known as Manichaeism) and pervading our civilisation through and through, and particularly virulent in Marxism, its most high-minded exponents not excluded: to wit, the conviction that evil is beyond the scope of God's love and omnipotence, and that therefore, one day, 'the wicked will have to be destroyed'. Thérèse's whole life protests the opposite: 'All are chosen.' Yes, henceforth we can all accept ourselves and each other for what we are, because Christ loves us. Yes, a new sort of brotherhood is born under Christ's eye. And true rehabilitation, that of mercy, can take place, even for those who think of themselves as marginal, on the fringes of society or the Church, even those who think of themselves as far away, even for the Good Thief. Yes, God has put an end to evil, but not in the way that we are tempted to do it: by hiding it or by attributing it to someone else or other people. No, if God takes evil away, he first makes its presence evident, but he bears what he denounces, and he takes away what he bears. He takes it on himself in order to abolish it. He breaks the chain of endless expiations. Mercy produces a concentration of evil but, having produced it, has the power to remove the evil and not let it spread afresh.

Blessed are the useless

It caused a good deal of surprise that a Carmelite nun should be designated 'patroness of the missions'. There has been a lot of criticism. And so the following point has to be made.

Now of course Thérèse 'did' a great deal, by opening her mind, by keeping informed about what was going on from Saigon to Hanoi, by adopting missionary 'brothers', by offering her heroic acts of self-sacrifice for the salvation of those so far away, and so forth.

But all this is not the primary reason for her being more and more appropriately the patron saint of the missions. There is a simpler, stronger reason. She grasped the fact that Love had put her in the very birthplace of the Church, Christ's heart, giving her a share in the eternal source of all missionary endeavour: Christ's anguish during his life and passion over a people to be saved who refused to be saved. Henceforth, no one has the right to think of any one of his fellow-men as marginal to this anguish. And by the same token, we are all part of the 'mission'. . . . since we all of us refuse.

So here again, thanks to her 'discoveries', Thérèse obliges us to change our normal way of looking at things. She instinctively grasped the New Testament's deepest insights into the nature of the 'mission'. When, in St John's Gospel, Christ gives the credentials for his work, he always does this by reference to its origin: 'those whom the Father has entrusted me with are most precious of all', 'what the Father has made known to me, I have made known to you'. In the first place, he is sent 'from the Father'. Similarly St Paul and the author of the Epistle to the Hebrews describe themselves first of all as ambassadors, that is, people who function on behalf of the person they represent and from whom they come. The same feature, in Acts, characterises the choice of the apostle who was to replace Judas: he was to be selected from those who had 'lived with Christ' and been 'witness of the Resurrection'.

So too Thérèse constantly expressed herself like that. Her letter to Céline of 15 August, 1892 is a perfect example: 'One day when I was wondering what I could do to save souls, some words in the Gospel gave me a sudden insight. . . . "Raise your eyes.". . . He doesn't wish to do anything without involving us.'

We might re-design the standard picture of Thérèse: not with eyes lowered to snap up every available piece of information, but 'raising her eyes to Christ's work'. For Thérèse, 'the apostolate'—that of prayer and of her life—didn't consist in analysing the needs of mankind (others had the job of doing that) nor in devouring information etc. It consisted in penetrating the needs of God, God's need to spread life and love on earth, his need to choose himself children to make up the 'empty places' in his Kingdom. This reversal of the normal view may strike us as irritating . . . But isn't it, once again, the only evangelical one, fully justifying the designation of a 'useless' person as patroness of the missions?

Reviewing the period from 1889 to the closing weeks of 1897, it is impossible to get away from the radically theocentric quality of Thérèse's apostolic zeal. She receives her brothers from Christ as Christ had received them from his father, and this is the principal reason why 'they are most precious of all', beginning with Pranzini.

Thérèse understood that God is the only person by whom I have the certainty of knowing that I am fully known, accepted and loved. The only person who can reach me in the depths of solitude where inevitably I find myself on occasion to be. The only One whom, I am certain, shares completely in the pangs of living and dying and who, one day, sooner or later, will draw all men into his arms. In the Garden of Gethsemane, in Jesus of Nazareth, God experienced this ordeal more acutely than any creature will ever experience it. So, under God's eye and in God's heart, I know that I can be myself, without pretence, without striking attitudes, without shame, without anger, since my own sin is crucified with him. What no one on earth can ever achieve, what no force on earth, whether political, social, pyschological or whatever, can do, God's mercy does—i.e. allows every individual to be himself, freely, without the feeling that he is being judged but, quite the reverse, that he is accepted with his burden of grandeur and misery, of nobility and cowardice, of self-forgetfulnes and self-absorption, to liberate us from all fear, from the fear of evil. This is how God loves: he reaches us where no human being can reach us.

'God's glory is the living man', said St Irenaeus in the early days of Christianity. By giving us back the true face of God and by helping us to believe—to the last—in the triumph of mercy for all, Thérèse, now more than ever before, serves and bears witness to his true glory, the glory of Love.

9

GLORY AND THE BEGGAR

On 7 June 1897, two days before learning for certain that her death was near, Thérèse, worn out by illness, posed on her knees in the cloister at Lisieux to have photographs taken. They were to be the last. One of them, showing a twenty-four-year-old face, looking fifty, is the most fascinating of all, allowing us a glimpse of what it was like in the Garden of Gethsemane. A year earlier, the same pose: Thérèse held a lily. Fine. This time she is holding—you might say, offering for the last time—two pictures: the Child Jesus and the Holy Face.

Has this some bearing on the 'glory' of God?

Mother Agnes was perfectly right when she gave as the reason for Thérèse's beatification: 'The glory of God, principally by proclaiming his mercy.' That is to say, by once again revealing God's true face: the face of the Christian God, of the God of the Gospel, after all the distortions which human hardness of heart had attributed to it over the centuries. Thérèse is central to the modern Church, because she knows that these distortions, which are more unjust and terrifying than even our attitudes to our fellow-beings, do not represent God's true face.

Neither useful nor useable

Note first of all a curious reversal, one which we are all invited to make. Thérèse seeks and discovers this face in the name of love, not in that of ideas: the face of a Child, of an Innocent Man condemned, the Holy Face. Now, you do not 'use' a child or an innocent. . . .

It is no different for us than it was in the days of Abraham and of Jesus. God, in the name of what he is, Love, confounds even our religious aspirations when these are misdirected. We may choose to be deaf. . . . The God of Moses, of David, of St John, of St Paul, of Francis of Assisi, of Thérèse of Lisieux, is disconcerting, bewildering at first in that he is not to be sought in the realm of the useful or usable. Since the coming of Jesus Christ, he is no longer content to be reduced to playing a role—and we gradually have to convince ourselves of this—either as the guarantor of world order, or as guardian of the social order or of morality, or as a super-philosopher and defender of ideas, or as a super-engineer watching over the scenario and functioning of the universe. Neither judge, nor refuge. All the functions assumed by these gods have now been taken over by other people. We have to go back to the real beginning, and this inevitably entails a wrench which no one else can go through on our behalf. this is always an 'ordeal'. That same which is the hallmark of love. No one who loves can bring himself to treat the beloved as an object of satisfaction, or be treated like that himself. The God of Jesus Christ never manifests himself as though he were going to overwhelm us in the way that one might respond to some need. He never manifests himself as the substitute for what we lack. He is much more. So much more that he can only offer himself to us in destitution and beggary.

So, as in all true love, the recognition and encounter with the one we love can really only take place under the aspect of a kind of dying, a dying caused by a self-transcending love: the refusal to treat the beloved as something disposable or useful to oneself. God's response—as we may well imagine—involves a certain wrench before we can hear it: the God of faith is beyond the useful or useless, in the silence of adoration, and this silence can on certain occasions be very hard to hear.

Here, we are at the very heart of Thérèse's revolutionary intuition about the Church (and it really was a revolution, after three centuries of Jansenisn had exacted their toll). She sums it up in a letter to Céline: 'He was silent before his judges! . . . He became poor so that we could be charitable to him. Like a beggar, he stretches out his hand to us, so that on the radiant Day of Judgement he will be able to say those wonderful words to us: "Come, you blessed of my Father, for I was hungry and you gave me food." Jesus Christ himself said these words and he it is who wants and begs for our love. He puts himself as it were at our mercy. He doesn't wish to take anything unless we give it to him. And the smallest trifle is precious in his divine eyes.' This idea seemed extraordinary in the Church of her day, although it was a truth which had always been taught; but now, suddenly, here was somebody actually practising it to the last.

God has disarmed for ever. And since Calvary, every Gospel and every Mass has been telling us the same thing. God has resigned the image of himself to us. God has taken love to such a point of delicacy as to let us model his face. This is the 'folly' of the Incarnation. Consequently, when history comes to an end, whereas we shall have to thank God for everything, paradoxically God himself will be able to thank us too. The secret of Thérèse's joy and her intuition about 'heaven' is this: that, in response to her love, God will allow her to share his omnipotence: 'I was hungry. . . . You gave me. . . . Are you willing? Now it's my turn!'

Not an idea, not an idol, God is the disarmed presence of someone alive, living in our life, an 'Incarnation' in daily life, not the pure but empty austerity of an idea, nor the illusion of an idol, but a disarming presence because disarmed, the presence of love: a child, an innocent. This was the decisive and bewildering way in which God chose to manifest himself once and for all in Jesus Christ. That something extraordinary would happen could be foreseen throughout Israelite history, but exactly what no one could imagine before the days of Jesus Christ. How can God show that he is the Altogether Other, that he is God? By his might, by his power to organise, by dogmatic certitude, by repressiveness? No, no, by helplessness and weakness, the helplessness and weakness of love. 'I cannot fear a God who has made himself so little for my sake—I love him, for he is only love and mercy!' This is the God tormented by human misery and seemingly powerless. Only Jesus, Jesus Christ crucified, the Holy Face raised at the centre of the world, would make it even possible to suspect this: a distinct face, a God whose face is unlike any other, because he is God. Origen in the early days of Christianity exclaimed, 'It is dangerous to talk about God'. Yes, it is—about this God, since he has laid down his arms. And for us, this face is the only one absolutely different from anything that creatures can tell us: the face of the folly of the cross, which Thérèse discovered early on in life and went on discovering all her life.

'Are you willing?'

To put it schematically, this is what we could say:
—the God of the philosophers, the God of science and nature: 'Things are what they are; there is existence and order; there is chance and necessity; seek and find';

—the God of the aesthetes: 'Wait and you will see, be patient and you will find Wisdom';
—the God of the moralists: 'You ought, we must. This is your duty';
—the God of the ideologists: 'What have you built? what are you fighting for?'

But all the God of Jesus has to say, all the God of Thérèse has to say, in history and in our daily lives, is: 'Are you willing?' Disarmed and disarming: 'Are you willing?'

Are you willing, like the prodigal son, to rely on another image of yourself and so recover hope? Are you willing, like Zacchaeus and Mary Magdalen, to look beyond your guilt? Attuned to the Beatitudes, are you willing to take the poor man in, to suffer for righteousness, peace, mercy? Are you willing not to be afraid of weeping? Are you willing to entrust me with your past and future? Are you willing? And lastly, are you willing to have me? Are you willing to lead your life with me, the real life, the life of hoping and giving, of truth and joy? No longer us, then, purifying our ideas or inventing our idols, no longer us seeking God by the light of our own courage, our own notions: but God, God himself, with Jesus's face, embodied in the concrete events of daily life, coming looking for us and asking this one question: 'Are you willing, are you willing to make your life a partnership with me? Are you willing?'

'He is thirsty for love'

God's beggary: we must not confuse this insight with the Nestorian concept of 'God's vulnerability' or its recent approximations about God's weakness. If God's beggary expresses the essence of Christianity, this is because it is inspired by love and by what is the very essence of love in its pure state: the need to be reciprocated.

'That is all Jesus asks of us. He has no need of our works, only of our love. For that same God who declares that he has no need to tell us if he is hungry, isn't ashamed to beg a drop of water from the Samaritan woman. He was thirsty. But in saying, "Give me something to drink", the Creator of the universe was asking for his poor creature's love. He was thirsty for love. Oh, I know, now Jesus is thirstier than ever; among the world's disciples all he meets is ingratitude and indifference, and among his own disciples he finds, alas, few hearts to give themselves unreservedly to him, few to understand the full extent of his infinite love.' In 1895, Thérèse wrote: 'I understand better than before how much Jesus yearns to be loved.' She had understood this for a long time. But in June 1895, when she was inspired to offer herself to Merciful Love, she understood it *better than before.*

Where is the threshold?

There is a threshold in every Christian life. And this threshold, we can unhesitatingly say, is that decisive moment when we are sure of being loved, and of being loved in an exceptional way. And here we use the word threshold in the sense that the threshold conditions the whole house, as in the case of an Alpine chalet for instance. An aperture perfectly orientated towards the sun, protected from the north wind, constructed of the best available stone, the threshold gives access to the whole house: sittingroom, cowshed, washhouse, stairs to the hayloft, bedrooms. If the threshold is wrongly aligned, the light throughout the house is diminished. The threshold is where you stand, where you greet, where you rest and where you talk.

'The only thing that counts is not what human beings want or try to do, but the mercy of God' (Rm 9:16). 'I shall not call you servants any more, because a servant does not know his master's business; I call you friends, because I have made known to you everything I have learnt from my Father' (Jn 15:15). This is how St Paul and St John define where the threshold of Christianity lies: we are loved and invited to enter into partnership with God's friendship.

Now, however we may describe friendship, we can, following Thomas Aquinas, distinguish three essential factors without which friendship cannot exist: 1. it is a love, not self-seeking, but seeking the good of the beloved; 2. it is a love based on exchange; 3. but for this love to be 'friendship' properly speaking, the exchange must be concerned with the love itself. And it is this third factor, *reciprocity*, which is the essential element in the definition.

Of its nature, love can remain one-sided. And this indeed is the element of suffering in any love-affair: Does the other love me as much as I love him? Why doesn't he answer? What does his silence mean? We all know how painful this uncertainty can be, and we all also know that this is the source and threshold of all joy and bliss for the lover. The exchange may have originally started with something or other held in common: a sharing of taste, of activity, of attitude. But something radically new occurs when the attachment is born of and nourished by the certainty that the other loves because we love him. Knowing that we are for the other person what that other person is for us, in terms of love, that is, and knowing that he wants our love, that he needs it, that he 'begs' for it.

When Christ discards the notion of servant in favour of that of friend, he does this to get rid of all reasons external to this sharing of love. 'As I have loved you': the reciprocity of love between man and God originates in, is modelled on, the life of God himself. We know how Nygren, the great Swedish Protestant theologian, attempted to define charity in terms of human love and its two opposing tendencies: *eros* and *agape*, acquisitive love and oblative love. But this definition falls short. The model for Christian love is not to be found in man but in the life of God. Charity confers not merely a difference of degree on love, but a difference of nature. Since the coming of Christ, we are all faced with something radically new, in that we can no longer go on explaining our destiny in terms of ourselves. For us to understand ourselves, we are now obliged to define ourselves in terms of God's life. Either we have to accept this—and the key to doing so is this reciprocity of love—or we have to suppress the essential message of the Gospel.

Reciprocity or nothing

Christ doesn't love us because of some community of interest or external activity but because of what we are to him. What the Father says to him: 'This is my beloved son in whom I am well-pleased,' is what he wants to say to us: 'As the Father has loved me, so I have loved you.' This is the decisive difference, the decisive threshold of our lives: loving Christ as someone waiting for the joy of being loved by us. God wishes to do his work in response to his friends. That primal episode of the pastoral charge to St Peter beside the lake after the resurrection was not first and foremost a call to responsibility, to courage, to initiative, to a better use of his brains in the future. It was a call to reciprocity: 'Peter, do you love me?' Thrice repeated: 'Peter, do you love me more than these?' (Jn 21:15-17). This was the only certainty on which Peter's life could be effectively based and which could justify what was to follow: 'Somebody else will put a belt round you and take you where you would rather not go' (Jn 21:18). St Paul was to say exactly the same thing, 'I live now not with my own life but with the life of Christ who lives in me' (Gal.

2:20). 'In your minds you must be the same as Christ Jesus' (Ph. 2:5). We might give many examples of this reciprocity's being lived in the history of the Church. Take this, for instance, as one of the most powerful ones, related in the Acts of the Martyrs: Perpetua and Felicity were in prison and about to be thrown to the lions, despite their youth. Felicity was on the point of giving birth. When the child was born, she cried out. One of her gaolers said to her: 'If you scream now, what will you do in the amphitheatre once the beasts start biting?' 'Don't worry about that,' said Felicity. 'Someone else will be suffering in me then.'

Man proposes, God disposes?

You may object that I am reducing charity to sentimentality. No, I reply. Without this actual reciprocity in love—which is known as the Holy Spirit—the Christian life just won't hold together. 'For me to love you as much as you love me, I shall have to borrow your love; then alone shall I find repose.' In saying this, Thérèse expresses the ultimate message of the Gospel—God has put himself at our disposal, God gives God to man.

For years, I used to admire a motto often to be seen in the chalets of the High Alps. On the king-post holding up the roof, you often find the words: 'Man proposes, God disposes.' I used to think of this as an act of faith. So it is. Now, however, the formula doesn't strike me as 'Christian'. He who would dispose, in the sense that we had no alternative but to submit, might well be a force but would not be God. I shouldn't want that for a father. A father is the opposite of someone who disposes; he is the one who inspires, awakens and promotes freedom and creativity in those to whom he gives life. What would be the point of giving life, if not to love in the other that difference by which the latter in turn becomes a source of love? Hence, for the formula to be 'Christian', it has to be put the other way round: 'God proposes and man disposes.'

'Even if God were to kill me'

From this we can grasp the reason for Thérèse's incredible daring. She gets it from this deep-down reciprocity: 'You love St Augustine

and St Mary Magdalen, souls whose sins were forgiven because they
had loved much (Lk 7:47). I love them too, I love their repentance
and more than anything else their loving boldness! When I see the
Magdalen stepping out from among all those guests and sprinkling
her Master's feet with her tears, I know that her heart had understood the abyss of love and mercy in Jesus's heart and that, sinful
woman as she was, that loving heart was not only ready to forgive
her but actually to lavish the benefits of his divine intimacy on her
and raise her to the highest peaks of contemplation.

'Since it was given to me to understand the love in Jesus's heart
too, I tell you, it has driven all fear from my heart! The memory of
my faults humbles me and leads me never to rely on my own
strength—which is but weakness—but, even more, the memory
speaks to me of mercy and love. When, in absolute filial trust, we
throw our faults into the devouring furnace of Love, how can they
possibly not be burnt away once and for all?'

This was not mere rhetoric. Thérèse wrote this when she knew
herself doomed to die. In the month of July, at the darkest moment
of her descent towards death, she was to say: 'The words of Job,
"Yes, though God kill me, yet will I hope in him", have delighted
me ever since I was a child. But it took me a long time to reach such
a state of abandonment. Now I have done so; God has brought me to
it, he has taken me in his arms and put me there.' Shortly before her
profession as a nun, at the age of seventeen, she had already voiced
this boldness born of reciprocity in one of the most extraordinary
sentences ever pronounced: 'He will get tired of making me wait for
him long before I get tired of waiting for him!'

Anticipating glory

This realisation that God becomes a beggar for the sake of reciprocity of love not only gave Thérèse the boldness of the saints but was
the unifying factor of her life. No longer was she primarily, or exclusively, concerned with renunciation and self-sacrifice, but with
responding to the good pleasure of the One who loves her. Which, you might
say, is the best way of expressing the radical novelty of Christian life
led *according to the paschal mystery*. Knowing God, living according to
Christ, means entering *a new order of existence*, of which Another is
centre and light. Few beings can have lived their lives as an *anticipa-
tion of the glory to come*, in the way that Thérèse did. And this is surely

one of the most original features of her witness. And this must surely be why many of our Orthodox brothers find it so easy to identify with her. By faith, we are called to something much greater than humanism, to something much greater than the re-creation of a lost paradise or of an 'integral' human nature by means of grace. By faith, we are invited to transcend ourselves, to become sons of God—to enter a new state, that of becoming divine ourselves.

With the coming of Christ into the world and the completion of the paschal mystery, a new element was introduced into the human condition, something that cannot be merely defined in terms of the coming of grace or by a theology of grace. Christ and the accomplishing of the paschal mystery brought a new quality of life into the world, introducing an entirely new psychology, that of glory. By dying on the cross and rising again, Christ received the power of communicating this glory not only to his own body but to all those who were to enter into communion with his post-resurrectional life. And this is something absolutely new: a participation, in the darkness of faith, in Christ's life, eating simultaneously at the Father's table and at the sinners' table. And this involves a wrench, something also new in the history of human psychology, since man is now participating in God's life.

This was what Thérèse lived with such astounding intensity. This was the source of her incredible hope: the explanation of and key to any understanding of her very personal approach to the Christian mysteries, i.e. always in terms of what they are to someone else, Christ; always as the expression of the good pleasure of someone who loves her. Be it prayer, the eucharist, brotherly love, institutions, her vocation, and so forth, everything is seen in terms of an exchange, of a response, of inter-subjectivity. And this changes everything's meaning. Hence her frequent references to 'heaven', not as future reward, but as present source of life, now, contemporaneous with her faith. How well she grasps that true eschatology: her ultimate point of reference is glory, Christ alive today, in whose existence she participates by faith, allowing her to see all things as God sees them! And for her, this alone removes all ambiguities arising from actual practice, from the shortcomings of institutional religion, or from the shortcomings of the orthodoxy of the moment.

Things only make sense for Thérèse in terms of a response to God:
—her vocation: 'Opening the Holy Gospel, I came on these words: "He called those to him whom it pleased him to call." This is the very mystery of my vocation, of my entire life indeed. He doesn't call those who are worthy of being called, but those whom he

pleases.' 'Perfection consists in doing his will, in being what he
wants us to be.'

—prayer: 'I can't say that I have often received consolations during my acts of thanksgiving; in fact, that is probably when I have
had least. I find this perfectly natural, since I offered myself to Jesus,
not as someone desiring him to visit me for my consolation, but
contrariwise as desiring to please him, he having given himself to
me.'

—in suffering and brotherly love. We have already mentioned
this, but let us make the point again. She is clear about the duty of
loving our neighbour. She knows by heart and quotes the apposite
passages in the Gospel. She knows the disappointments that arise,
either from her side or from others, when the time comes to translate
this into action. Her extreme sensitivity reacts to everything:
whether it be to the people who teach her the catechism, to her
superiors in the convent, to her fellow-nuns, to her family. Hence the
natural temptations to febrility or revolt. She explains her mind in
Chapter 10 of *The Story of a Soul*: charity is indissociably part of the
order of 'doing', concrete, practical, demanding, and of the order of
'looking', of sharing in the way Christ looks at things. And this
sharing or communion is what comes first: a matter of responding to
the will of someone else because he loves me, and hence of attaching
more value to what I ought to do because he expects and begs this of
me. 'Everything I have done has been to please God.' 'I have given
him everything. For a long while now I have not belonged to myself.
I have given myself totally to Jesus. He is free to do whatever he likes
with me.' In a period when a great many Christians used to keep
careful account of their virtuous deeds in the hopes of earning a
reward commensurate with their merits, Thérèse loved without
keeping account, prodigally, giving with both hands: 'When you
love, you don't keep count.' Her whole attitude can be summed up
in this: 'I'm not selfish. I love God, not me.' Love expressed in gems
of truly childlike sincerity, familiarities astounding and utterly out of
keeping with the atmosphere of a nineteenth-century Carmel.
Against the fear paralysing her companions, Thérèse protested: 'I
don't understand souls who are afraid of such a loving Friend.'
'Since it was given to me to understand the love in Jesus's heart, it
has driven all fear from my heart.' 'Ah, the Lord is so good to me
that I find it impossible to be afraid of him.' 'How can you expect me
to be afraid of someone whom I love so much?' Since God is truly her
Father and since she is truly his child, why shouldn't she call him
'Papa'? 'If—although it's impossible—God didn't see my good

actions, I shouldn't be worried in the least. I love him so much that I should like to be able to please him without his even knowing that it was I.'

Freedom of heart

'To please him': behind this almost infantile expression lies the most advanced form of self-abandonment and trust, and the strongest affirmation of the reality and immediacy of her faith. Thérèse lives for Christ living today in glory. This in no way diminishes the violence of the battle, but she fights knowing that victory is already won. Hence her constant effort never to allow the purity of her faithful regard to become tarnished and, to prevent this from happening, never to allow her freedom of heart to be impaired, or if so to reconquer it. In a word, to keep her heart free to love. A matter of staying free at all times to be able to recognise Love: whether behind the face of her humiliated father (especially in 1889-92); or behind the face—maternal though often disfigured by passion (jealousy)— of her Mother Prioress Marie de Gonzague; or behind the even more maternal but also humiliated face of Mother Agnes of Jesus, her sister (while the latter for instance held office as Prioress between 1893 - 6 and Thérèse was obliged to fortify her heart against natural compassion when Mother Marie de Gonzague was giving Mother Agnes a hard time; or behind the humiliated face of her other sister, Céline, whom Thérèse regarded as her *alter ego*, almost indeed as her child, and whose first steps in the religious life (1894-7) had been fairly disastrous and hence humiliating for Céline and so for Thérèse too.

Through all these everyday events, Thérèse had to recognise the presence of Love, not this or that kind of love but that Love 'the property of which is self-abasement'. Perhaps this is the ultimate reason for the 'contemplative' life: God has honoured us by allowing us to share the thought of Christ, and henceforth we are invited to see everything through Christ's eyes. Sublime yet concrete contemporaneousness of the Christian and the Gospel! The immediacy of that 'Advocate's' intercession, who is now interceding for us. 'It has pleased him to call us to his wonderful Light.' It is henceforth forbidden for us to harbour doubts about the purpose of our life, we no longer have the right to underrate it. God needs our love just as he needs his Son, and this is no longer optional now that he has decided and has decided for all eternity. We have the very real power of giving it to him in ourselves and, if we refuse, this is one gift from the Son to the Father which doesn't take place—not however that the eternal gift can ever cease. 'I have called you friends.' God has only one love, and when he loves, this is the only love he can give. The Father wants to re-live with us what occurs between his Son and himself; the gift of his Son to himself is the gift which he offers us. An offering which alone, in the final analysis, can reveal the why and wherefore of creation: 'a secret hidden from the wise and revealed to the little.'

Victim of justice or victim of love?

Among other documents of the period preserved in the Carmel at Lisieux is the announcement of the death of a Carmelite nun of the Luçon community, who died on Good Friday, 12 April 1895. The text is reproduced a little further on. The obituary is dated 30 May, 1895. Thérèse probably heard it read (in refectory or at recreation) before mass on Sunday, June 9, or in any case before drawing up her Act of Self-offering to Merciful Love, which she recited on 11 June 1895. A comparison of the notice with what Thérèse was to write is very significant: the one is the very antithesis of the other!

The basic difference is not between 'fear' and 'trust'—this being merely the consequence. The essential difference lies in what motivated the entire orientation of their two lives. For Thérèse, it wasn't primarily a matter of paying, suffering, making sacrifices and so forth, but of allowing love to respond to love. Hence we might express the entire rationale of her life in the following sequence:

—love lives by reciprocity; loving means accepting that he who loves me must give me the wherewithal to respond to him;

—Thérèse discovers this reciprocity by seeing how, despite his power, the Other refuses and denies himself the right to exert pressure, and instead invariably presents himself as a 'beggar': whence are born freedom and trust, whence again victory over all fear:

—this leads her to take him whom she loves as her source and support;

—whence the entire orientation of her life, i.e. the offering of herself in response to Love's 'begging'.

As the Theresean scholar Fr A. Patfoort observes: 'It is precisely when confronted by God's self-abasement that Thérèse, like St Paul

and St John, becomes certain of her power, by God's grace, to
dispose of God's very heart, of God's very love, to love him as he
himself loves her. 'O Trinity, you are the prisoner of my love.' 'The
favour of flying towards the Sun of Love on the very wings of the
Divine Eagle.' Thérèse is in fact re-using, in stronger and simpler
form, the very expressions of her master, St John of the Cross, where
he describes the inebriating awareness of being enabled to give God
to God.

'But, by the little way, Thérèse very rightly perceived that hope,
based on reciprocity of love, offers little ones this possibility long
before the ultimate stage of transforming charity is reached.'

This perhaps is the secret of her self-offering. But before we listen to
what she has to say, let us consider a few passages from the necrology which she heard at about the time she was drawing up her Act of
Self-Offering. The deceased nun in question was Sr Marie-Anne, a
Carmelite of Luçon:

To the end of her earthly career she preserved that same ardour for expia-
tion and suffering . . . All I can say is that our dear departed Sister ardently
desired to glorify God and to save souls. With this aim, she sought suffering
and frequently offered herself as a victim to Divine Justice . . . To obtain the
conversion of a member of her family, she deprived herself completely of
fruit for a whole year. To convert a poor sinner who had been commended to
her, she made a resolution never again to eat butter as long as she lived,
although she was very fond of it . . . Last July, as in previous years, our
beloved Sister made her major retreat at the same time as the priests of the
diocese, with intensified fervour and desire to purge herself of her imperfec-
tions, so that she might go to Heaven without first passing through Purgatory. Thereafter the thought never left her; in her retreat resolutions we find
the following notes: 'Implore our Lord to avenge sin on me and make me
suffer pains and ordeals, according to his good pleasure, for the needs of the
Church and the salvation of souls . . . so that I may go, without delay, to
bless, adore, love and glorify God in eternal bliss.'
     Though her sufferings grew more acute, she bore them with great pati-
ence, even desiring to suffer more, to complete the purgation of her soul on
earth. She also ardently desired to die on a Saturday, so that she might enjoy
the privilege of the Sabbatine Bull . . . Let us indeed hope that her prayer
was heard, for she breathed her last on Friday evening, after First Vespers of
Saturday. . . .
     At last the great day came—day of mercy and justice, of grief and love. All
her life she had known little but the consolations and raptures of love, but
now came the time for her to experience its purging and ever-merciful trials.
On her dying lips, we heard the frequent cry, gasped out in anguish, 'I'm
enduring the rigours of Divine Justice . . . Divine Justice . . . Divine Jus-

tice ... O Jesus! come quickly, quickly. I can't endure any more ... I
accept these inner torments ... Uncertainty ... uncertainty ...' Raising
and looking at her cold and trembling hands, she said: 'I don't have enough
merits. I must acquire more.'

From two till three o'clock on Good Friday afternoon, the struggle was
terrible. . . .

We hope that our dearly beloved Sister, so fully trusting in divine mercy,
may have received a favourable welcome before the Sovereign Judge; but
since the Lord's judgements are impenetrable, we pray you of your kindness
to add your prayer to those already requested.

A few days after hearing or reading this necrology, Thérèse was to
offer herself, not to Justice, but to Merciful Love. There is nothing to
add to what she herself says about it, except that every Christian is
called to make the same response, to practise the same reciprocity,
even if he doesn't know it or cannot do it. Thérèse reminds us
categorically that high-mindedness isn't what is required, but
trust—which anyone can manage:

'This year, on 9 June, the feast of the Holy Trinity, I received the
grace of understanding better than before how much Jesus desires to
be loved.

'I was thinking about those souls who offer themselves as victims
to the Justice of God, to deflect and draw down on themselves the
punishments in store for the guilty. This offering seemed grand and
noble-hearted to me, but I felt far from being drawn to make it. "O
my God!" I exclaimed in the depths of my heart, "is your justice
alone to receive souls self-sacrificed as victims? Doesn't your Merciful Love need victims too? On all sides it is ignored and rejected; the
hearts on whom you long to lavish it turn away to love of other
creatures, seeking happiness from these with their miserable affection, instead of throwing themselves into your arms and accepting
your infinite Love. O my God, is your despised Love to remain
locked up in your heart? I think, if you were to find souls offering
themselves as burnt-offerings to your Love, you would swiftly consume them; I think you would be glad at not having to repress the
waves of infinite tenderness within you. . . If your Justice loves to be
done, though it extends only to earth, how much more must your
Merciful Love long to burn up souls, since your Mercy is as high as
Heaven ... O my Jesus, let me be that happy victim! Consume
your burnt-offering with the fire of your Divine Love!" '

What could we venture to add? Except to read Thérèse's Act of
Self-Offering over again. And have the courage while reading it to
pray that it may become ours, and to accept the silence which alone
is worthy of such boldness—the silence of the Beggar.

CONCLUSION
THE DUTY OF BEING HAPPY

'I find holiness repellant'

'A saint is a dead man; though in the world, he no longer belongs to the world. The Church still canonises, though without enthusiasm; the faithful themselves have an obscure feeling that saints belong to the past. I find holiness repellant, with its sophistries, its rhetoric and its morose delectation; it serves only one purpose today: of allowing dishonest men to advance worse arguments' (Jean-Paul Sartre in *Saint Genêt*).

Well, yes, I would reply, Sartre may very well be right, but only on one condition: holiness not only can but should repel us if the saints in question haven't been happy and haven't increased the sum of human happiness. If such is the case, Sartre is right. If not, he is arguing on the side of unhappiness. Thomas Aquinas ends his treatise on God by meditating on God's happiness, and opens his treatise on Man (and all human morality) with a study of happiness. What about Thérèse? Can she help us to understand this more clearly? In spite of everything we may be told about her 'little way', about her discovery of hope, about her trust, about our all being called, especially if we are ungifted, weak or sinful, this doesn't prevent her life of suffering and renunciation from making us feel afraid. Yes, it is frightening. Would as much eventually be asked of us? Safer perhaps not to know too much about it.

'What had this battle got to do with me?'

'It's true, she said, I ought to have been more prudent, seeing that I had nothing to give. Oh, these aren't things you'll find easy to understand and I doubt if I can make you see what my motives were! Deep down, all I thought about was God; I was only simple and cheerful for his sake ... a child, a little child. Men are sad, so sad! Does this strike you as strange? I spent years and years learning that, imagine it! We are so used to it that we don't notice how sad men are. I didn't want to believe it; I was like people who connive in looking cheerful when talking to invalids. Yes, indeed, there is the joy of God, joy in a word—each of us has his own idea of that.... But the saints, the greatest saints, know the secret of letting it show without harming their neighbour. What had this battle of men got to do with me? I only succeed at easy things. And because I never attempt anything else, people imagine that I can do anything, expecting miracles of me....

'And however unhappy I may be one day, sadness will have no part in me, ever ... Sin? We are all in sin, some of us enjoy it and others suffer because of it, but when all's said and done, we are all breaking the same bread beside the fountain, holding back our saliva—the same disgust. You were certainly wrong to expect anything from me. But I give you what I've got, what little I've got, neither more nor less. I don't want to defend myself any more, that's over. We have no right to defend ourselves.... God doesn't keep any of us like valuable birds in an aviary. He gives his best friends away, gives them away for nothing—to the good, to the bad, to everyone, as he was given away by Pilate! "Here, take him, this is the man." My word, Sir, in that carnival of soldiers, priests and painted whores, what a strange affair humanity's first communion was!'

Is Bernanos also putting forward a bad argument, as Sartre would have it, in this passage from *La Joie*, where without actually saying so, he is in fact writing about Thérèse of Lisieux?

Alone with our freedom

Marcel Moré, writing about Thérèse in *La foudre de Dieu*, has exactly grasped what lies at the core of her witness:
'In modern times, sacral society has collapsed, the world has begun to disintegrate, the gifts of the Holy Spirit have been put to flight. A grandiose world nonetheless, since everything has vanished and man is alone in it, totally denuded, alone with his freedom, confronting a God who has stripped himself of his power. Man is

reduced to such a state of misery that all he can do now is wait for the unexpected from God, while God for his part waits for him to make the loving gesture of humbling himself. But in this world, the horizon is as though walled off in all directions; the wind of science has raised the wind of despair, so that it seems as though the Redemption had been a failure. Our world's heart is overflowing with bitterness and sadness, not in the way it might if we were bored, but because, it seems, the Blood flowing from that 'pierced and bleeding hand' no longer has a divine or redemptive character. And, just as Franciscanism was for many centuries, thanks to *The Little Flowers of St Francis*, the symbol of joy in suffering, *so now in the basically metaphysical sadness of the modern age, Thérèse by a mysterious design of Providence, has had as vocation, among other things, that of taking everything on herself under the guise of joy and consolation.*

'Even so, we must understand the real significance of her "looking cheerful". When people of my generation went to catechism (at roughly the time when Thérèse was dying her "death of love" in the convent infirmary), we were taught that a Christian had a duty to look cheerful, so as to encourage others in the way of heroism. But this was not at all the case with Thérèse: she recognised herself to be not a strong woman but a very weak one. And the last thing she would have wished would have been to play the hypocrite. Her "appearance" of joy, which it seems she very rarely abandoned, even while writing *The Story of a Soul* under obedience or personal letters for reasons of affection and friendship, was simply a fence which she raised between herself and other people, so as to remain alone in the darkness with the mysterious Beggar. An essential condition for "consoling" Jesus, as she constantly repeats, is silence, solitude and oblivion.

Oh, to console you, I wish
To live ignored on earth,

she wrote in one of her poems, and in another:

I want to suffer, saying nothing,
So that Jesus may be consoled.

'In the most "joyous" pages of *The Story of a Soul*, in the *Last Conversations* and in the *Letters*, she does her best, in a spirit of humility, to efface the memory of the Thérèse of the Depths, who had so truly written that the way to wipe away Jesus's tears was suffering "uncourageously", "sadly", with him.

'This sadness however is perfectly compatible with the "peace beyond all understanding" spoken of by St Paul. It happened that twice in less than a month during 1889, Thérèse would write of an "ineffable joy" beyond all joy. First, in a letter to Céline of 12 March, she writes that we shall be "deified at the very source of all joys and all delights", and then in a letter of 4 April, where she identifies this "ineffable joy" with peace (another of Thérèse's keywords). "To suffer in peace," she says, "you must really want everything that Jesus wants." But in fact, here she is writing about something beyond all joy and all suffering. This peace of the depths is God's joy, the beginning of our deification in the "darkness of exile", the ineffable.'

Starting all over again

It is very hard to write a life of Thérèse of Lisieux; there is too great a wealth of material. You have to follow a number of strands: charity, trust, prayer, desire for God.... You have to take note of her changes, or lack of change, of attitude to her environment, at peril of opposing or subordinating her to it.... You have to begin all over again at each 'decisive' moment: be it the Christmas conversion, the novitiate, the discovery of Scripture, her father's illness, the Act of Self-Offering. Each time there is a new beginning; at the same time you see that everything was there already, though now more deeply experienced.

The saints are artful, and Thérèse was a gifted one. To people who choose to believe that she despised the world, or that she was the victim of a mistaken dualism, or that she was a martyr to her own virginity, she has nothing to say. She hides. She does this, not to annoy us, not to get away from us, but to make us go all the way to the fountainhead, to what dominates us all: the search for happiness.

'Always cheerful and contented'

On 5 July 1897, four days before the really serious haemorrhages began, Thérèse said to her sister Agnes, 'Don't feel sad at seeing me ill, dear Mother, for you can see how happy God has made me. I am always cheerful and contented.'

Discussing Thérèse's optimism, P. Descouvement says: 'In point of fact, Thérèse didn't immediately discover how to convert her sufferings into joys. She made herself very plain about this on 31 July 1897. Some time after her first communion, she had asked the Lord to turn all earth's consolations into bitterness for her. She had found this prayer in *The Imitation of Christ* and was inspired to make it for fear of seeking in the plaudits and affections of "the world" that joy which she wished to find in God alone. The answer to it was not long to seek. The friendly overtures she made to this or that classmate were barely returned and many other trials overtook her. Yet, says Thérèse, "It didn't occur to me to take joy in this; that was a grace only accorded me later." But let us quote in full what she had to say, since this is one of the most important self-revelations that she ever made. "I have found happiness and joy on earth, but only in suffering—for I have suffered a great deal here below, and other people should be made aware of this ... Ever since my first communion, ever since I asked Jesus to turn all earth's consolations into bitterness for me, I have had a perpetual desire for suffering. But it didn't occur to me to take joy in this; that was a grace only accorded me later. Up to then, it was like a spark hidden under the ashes, and like a tree's blossoms destined ultimately to become fruit. But seeing my blossoms keep falling, i.e. allowing myself to burst into tears whenever I suffered, I used to think in sad bewilderment: This desire will never come to anything!"

'Later, Thérèse understood that, to suffer "according to God's heart", there was absolutely no need to suffer courageously, without seeming to notice her sufferings, as heroes and "spiritual giants" do. It was enough to accept her sufferings as they came and as she was, and to offer them to the Lord with all her heart, firmly believing that they were not useless. Thérèse had understood this completely while reading the retreat notes taken by Sr Marie of Saint Joseph during the retreat preached by Father Pichon at the Lisieux Carmel in October 1887. The meditation on Christ's agony, for instance, ended as follows: "God preserve us," some saint said, "from suffering grandly, strongly, high-mindedly! No, without the intimate cross of discouragement, believe me, all other crosses would be worthless." Thérèse had grasped the lesson perfectly, if the advice she sent to her sister Céline for her twentieth birthday, 26 April 1889, is anything to go by. "We mustn't imagine that we can love without suffering, without suffering a great deal.... Let's suffer bitterly, uncourage-

ously! Jesus suffered sadly. Unless sadly, would the soul suffer at all?
And yet we want to suffer high-mindedly, grandly! Céline, what a
foolish illusion!"

'And it was exactly in this way that Thérèse accepted suffering on
her sickbed. Suffering found her strengthless, joyless—no matter! As
she had already realised when she was sixteen, 'holiness doesn't
consist in fine sentiments, doesn't even consist in believing them or
feeling them. It consists in suffering and in suffering caused *by everything.*" ' (Les secrets de l'optimisme thérèsien', *Annales de sainte
Thérèse de Lisieux,* nos. 9 and 12).

'Am I suffering properly?'

One day Mother Agnes was congratulating her on her patience.
Thérèse replied: 'I haven't had a moment of patience yet. It's not *my*
patience! You are all mistaken.'

This was why Thérèse never asked God to increase her sufferings:
she was content to accept with a smile whatever suffering might be
presented, as witness this conversation of 26 August as related by Sr
Marie of the Eucharist in a letter to her father: 'She told us yester-
day, "Fortunately, I have never asked for suffering, for if I had, I
fear I might not have had the patience to endure it. However, since it
comes to me by the pure will of God, he cannot refuse me the
patience and grace I need to bear it." '

'No, God doesn't give me to expect an immediate death but greater suffering still,' she said on 23 August 1897, 'but I'm not worried
about that. I only want to think about the present.' 'I'm not the sort
to suffer over the past or suffer over the future. I only suffer in the
present moment. And so it's not so bad.' Thérèse said this on the day
when, racked with pain and temptation, she knew that she would
never again be able to receive communion. Two days earlier, she
said: 'I'm suffering a great deal, but am I suffering properly? That's
the question!' At the back of the book of Gospels which she invariably carried on her person, she had written:

Lord, you overwhelm me with joy
  By everything you do (Ps 16;5).

Why all this suffering?

One cannot help protesting at this point: why does God need all this suffering in order to make a saint? Isn't that the question underlying Sartre's sense of repugnance? Here we enter the final circle of hope. No one would dare to offer an answer. For the answer can't be framed in ideas and words. Only those who have passed through this circle can give it.

Thérèse has given her reply. For her, it wasn't a matter of suffering or of not suffering, but of preserving, come what might, the sweetness of love and peace of love. Christ on the Cross is certainly a 'tortured' being, but is first and foremost a being who loves his Father and mankind. If Christ was crucified, this wasn't to have us crucified too. It was to make us children. If we haven't the right to reply, we can and must try to understand, since this concerns the ultimate in all our lives—'ultimate' in the strongest sense, such as it had for the Greeks for instance, in that a treatise on Happiness inevitably dealt with the end, with the aim of human existence.

The duty of being happy

Happiness is one particular type of fulfilment: fulfilment of the spiritual being, for which purpose we were created. Hence the practial conclusion: *it is inevitable, legitimate and obligatory to seek happiness*. It was what Thérèse was to seek throughout her life. But we must not go looking in the wrong direction. For there is no immediate evidence to show that our true happiness is bound up with the right way we seek the will of God. Seeking fulfilment is certainly a 'duty', but hitting on the right way of doing this isn't a foregone conclusion. It's easy to make a mistake.

What is happiness? *The intense yet peaceful possession of everything we can desire.* Now, this totality isn't a matter of quantity. Satisfaction in possessing all is qualitatively distinct from pleasure and even joy. Thus in this sense, Christ's agony was at once a mystery of happiness and of suffering.

Peace and intensity : the co-existence of these two characteristics comprises the irreducible essence of happiness. Happiness is at once calm and violent. If one of these two characteristics is absent, then it isn't happiness any more. Life may be crowned with every satisfaction without being happy, or be perfectly calm and peaceful without being happy. Life, dynamism, inspiration, folly and, with these, wisdom, security, sweetness, inwardness: such are the two aspects of happiness. Movement and repose at the same time. Which is why we sometimes think we are dealing with irreconcilables; and tend to choose one or other of the paths—adventure or equilibrium. Hence the two great temptations, the two yearnings for happiness: on the one hand, all the Don Juans and Fausts, the lovers, the men of action who hope to find happiness in adventure, in the quest for action, love, art, drugs. We must always be moving on, ready, like Baudelaire, to ask death itself to take us no one cares where, so long as we find something new. And on the other, we seek happiness in the safety of equilibrium, the assurance of stable tenure, the joys of home.

Though people may incline to one or other of these aspects of happiness, all of them in fact need both. We all need happiness, and without both there is none. Those who run are racked by thirst to find a reality, an object, possession of which will eventually allow them to rest without losing their taste for intensity and novelty. The lovers of order and repose would like a fertile, living repose, not by any means a swoon or slumber. Each needs, whether this is admitted or not, a life forever new which will be repose, because simple, and intensity, because infinite. Hence the disappointment—taking on the form of the cross—once we discover we can never be satisfied by a created thing, unless we deliberately overlook its limitations or forget the violence of our thirst. 'God promises by his creatures, but only fulfils by himself,' wrote the youthful Claudel that same year that Thérèse entered the novitiate. The adventurers forget the limitations, bedazzled as they are by the objects of their satisfaction coming to them in ever swifter succession. The first shock reveals the splendour, but not the frontiers. Though there is indeed that split second of 'grace', when limitations can be forgotten, to give an illusion of the infinite. Having sucked the sweets, on to the next fruit! The unadventurous, in contrast, forget about their thirst and settle all too easily for a cut-rate happiness. They willingly compromise the true greatness of their lives, rather than be overtaxed by it— content to meet the sorrows of existence with stoic virtue.

Now, Thérèse accepted the thirst for happiness to the last. Across the years, she shouts to us that for a Christian to renounce the quest for happiness is sin.

The ordeal isn't what's fearsome

You can take one of three attitudes to the Beatitudes. You can reject them. You can reach an accommodation by only keeping what is liveable, possible, practicable. This can go on for a long time. You still have a life of your own, you still belong to yourself. This is bearable, but the danger is that you will eventually find that the Gospel becomes an oppressive yoke; you will have all the hardships of Christianity and virtue, without any of the joy. Which only leaves pursuing the Beatitudes without accommodating them. But who would dare? Who would not recoil before the cross? Doesn't this doctrine in fact propound that the only happiness possible is in the last resort impossible to attain?

Agreed, a great many doctrines passing themselves off as Christian do indeed lead us to this discouraging conclusion. But here too, Thérèse of Lisieux was vividly original: her instinctive faith preserved her from the fatal error of presenting the cross and ordeal as things external to true happiness. Looking at things from that angle, which is a tragically wrong one, we do indeed see the cross as standing on the road to happiness but seemingly *coming from outside*, as though to bar the way. Thérèse is more simple: for her, 'happiness' means loving someone, means loving all mankind. This being so, she can suffer anything and still be happy, if not superficially speaking, then at least essentially.

Throughout her life, Thérèse made a clear distinction between the mystery of the cross and the mystery of accepting divine life. This latter is far less terrifying to our imagination but is in fact the only fearsome mystery, since on it in the final analysis depends our salvation and our acceptance of the cross. The ordeal isn't what is fearsome, but the decision whether or not to accept, to assent to *loving to the last the kind of life which God is offering us*. What Judas refused wasn't the cross, but the laying down of his arms before forgiveness. It's no longer a question of being strong, but of being sufficiently humble for love to be able to triumph in our lives. *Now, our strength depends much less on ourselves than does our humility and weakness*; for Thérèse, this is the secret of happiness, and this is the secret of the Beatitudes. And love of our own excellence is precisely what always, and in the last resort only, puts us in jeopardy of saying, No, of feeling repelled by the infinite happiness offered us by God. Boldly we must say with Thérèse: the cross isn't the real difficulty, but the disarming of self by which we give ourselves to God.

Any offer of a new kind of life, any invitation to a journey, is fearsome. There is always that leap into the unknown (what Thérèse used at each stage to call 'darkness' or 'fog'). And however attractive that unknown may be, there is always the critical moment, that moment of transition, the passover from one kind of life to another, when you lose the security of the first without yet having got that of the second. When in Dostoievsky's *The Adolescent*, Katerina Nicolaievna answers Versiloff's 'Did you love me?'—'Yes.'—'Do you now?'—'No, I could have loved you if you had loved me less,' Katerina doesn't realise that she has just given away the secret of their entire relationship. She is right. This man can only offer her security. God offers us a life combining the infinite and repose.

And how can you have two happinesses at the same time? By consenting to accept the Gospel, we consent to enter a different order of existence. A life which becomes our life while remaining essentially someone else's life. From this standpoint we can see that the Beatitudes can only be understood if we are already *inside* the Kingdom. For—and here lies the paradox—they offer us happiness, not merely as opposed to false human wisdom, but even as opposed to true wisdom (1 Cor. 1:17—2:9). Their only justification lies in their fulfilment in God. They are at once declaration and promise. Declaration of fact: that of the new righteousness in which the cross's sinister aspects are no longer regarded as an obstacle; and promise—a no longer merely external one—that the Kingdom reverses the conditions on which happiness may be had. And in this sense, everything in the Gospel appears designed to teach us humility, poverty and meekness. And furthermore, as Thérèse was to re-discover, to teach us *to love* humility and poverty as requisite to divine happiness. We are disarmed, hence sure of victory.

We thirst for happiness but fear the thirst

We desire happiness but fear the cross. But happiness and the cross are mysteriously associated here on earth. For earthly happiness consists in loving, and love on earth is love crucified. Our happiness hence is a happiness crucified and hence a scandal. How shall we trace the Christian's progressive discovery of his vocation? Called to reach and share God's own bliss, he soon sees the cross rearing up in his path. Next, he discovers the cross isn't only an obstacle, but also a revelation of the bliss to which he is invited. He then begins to fear this bliss, at the same time continuing to desire it. And he cannot escape from either this fear or this desire, since he is at grips with an excessive love intent on taking possession of him.

Grace gives us the thirst for God, for God's bliss and no other kind. That alone can satisfy our craving, even though we may not know it. We may stay a long while without realising, may carry this germ about inside us for a long while without anything very much showing, just as we can carry a germ of life or a germ of death for years and years and go on leading an ordinary life without ever suspecting such a thing. At most, an obscure uneasiness may warn us that, despite a happy or thrilling life as commonly regarded, we are not satisfied; and then we find ourselves dreaming from time to time of something new, unexpected, extraordinary which never actually comes. Then, one day, the uneasiness becomes a call, an invitation to set out; we realise that down there and far away there is something waiting for us, and that this something is someone, and that this someone is God, God's bliss, a mystery which the eyes of man have not seen nor the ears of man heard, something unheard of and unfathomable. Then 'we leave Egypt' and set out in Christ's footsteps, like sheep following their shepherd, not in fact knowing where he is leading, since we know nothing whatever about this mysterious bliss in store for us. We only know that it is happiness, true happiness, our happiness, the happiness for which we were created, and that is all we want to know.

Between us and our happiness

In any case, the road is easy to begin with and we are enchanted by the journey itself. We have of course already read the Gospel and know that there are bound to be ordeals. But for the moment everything seems rosy, and ordeals can be dismissed as hypothetical— until the day when first we see the profile of the cross etched against the horizon. It is still a long way off, to be sure, and the obstacles giving us a foretaste of it are still probably light. Even so, the cross is no longer something imaginary, romantic, seductive, impersonal. It is standing in the path which we are treading and the path is leading us straight towards it. We truly realise then that it is the gate to that bliss for which we're bound and that, like Christ, we shall have to suffer and die to enter glory. The words of the Gospel and St Paul ring in our hearts with a new emphasis: 'If anyone wants to be my disciple, let him renounce self, take up his cross and follow me!'

Once these words have passed into our flesh and blood like this, how hard they are to bear! We are tempted to revolt against them, on those days when faith comes hardest. And we find them particularly hard to bear on the lips of people who do not always seem to have grasped their full import. Yet, that is the truth: between us and our happiness, the only happiness we really want, stands the cross, our cross, the only cross that we don't want to carry.

Then we start being alarmed at this disconcerting journey and feel inclined to cheat. We reassure ourselves as best we may. Sometimes we are weak and try to forget about the harshness of the message inscribed in our hearts. We are not short of fine axioms either: 'Grace doesn't destroy nature. Our duty is to embrace the modern world and spoil the Egyptians. Our times require an incarnate spirituality, we should beware of the other-worldly and mystagogic. Christian life is a fulfilling, not an amputation. We mustn't emasculate ourselves, we must hold on to human values . . .' Sometimes we feel strong and noble and then there is an even subtler temptation to dodge the real situation, one therefore that much harder to unmask. We screw up our courage, we whip ourselves up to heroic heights: 'After all, this is only a bad patch; let's make an effort and endure, for love of God, what so many others have endured for less creditable reasons; we can't do anything by ourselves, of course, but grace won't be lacking if we are faithful and resolute. Help yourself and God will help you. Let us run our race to carry off the prize. etc.'

The race is not to the strong

This is all very well, but the mystery of the cross is deeper than that; you can't get out of it by nobility, even assisted by grace. And this is the final and decisive stage which Thérèse helps us to pass through. It isn't particularly easy—and in another sense it isn't particularly difficult, since it isn't reserved to the strong, and the weakest can do it. It's much easier and much harder, since basically the mystery of the cross isn't a mystery of strength but a mystery of helplessness. It is a victory, to be sure, but a victory hidden even from the eyes of the victor, a victory having every appearance and all the taste of defeat, and experienced as a defeat. The cross isn't a mystery of bravery but a mystery of love. It doesn't consist in suffering courageously, nor merely in suffering, full-stop, but in being afraid of suffering; it doesn't consist in overcoming an obstacle but in being crushed by it;

not in being strong and noble-hearted but in being small and absurd in one's own eyes; not in deploying virtue but in seeing all one's virtues routed and pulverized; and in accepting all this lovingly. And in accepting lovingly to be strengthless; strength is no use, love is what's needed. So we shan't reach the goal by gritting our teeth since, if we are capable of gritting our teeth, this means that we are strong, and all the while we are strong—with this kind of strength—we still don't know what the cross is all about. Christ didn't grit his teeth to go to his Passion, he didn't pluck up his courage, he knew very well that he couldn't. He merely said: 'Father, your will be done, not mine', which is something of a different order, of a different world, the world of love. And not merely love of the human sort, but a love commensurate with God, of God's sort, that is to say, love of a sort we can never produce of ourselves. This sort of love isn't ours to give. God has to breathe it into us, he has to come into us to love himself.

Not the cross but God frightening us now

This divine love is eternal life already, the only aspect of eternal life which we can experience on earth. Faith and hope will pass away, but charity will not pass away. Hence it is a foretaste of eternal bliss, bliss on earth, the happiness of truly loving, of loving to excess, of loving as God loves. And this happiness is so little satisfying that it gives rise to an intense thirst to see God. We know that in heaven there will be no more shadows or tears and we naturally want to be there. But this isn't the blissful thirst of love: on this earth, we can never cease to thirst, thirsting for love or thirsting for God. But there is in love and in the very thirst which it engenders a certain presence of him whom we love which, even if we do not feel it and believe ourselves forsaken, is already a kind of bliss. In heaven we shall not yearn to love more: we shall only know desire for God, ever satisfied and ever renewed. But on earth, all the while we haven't attained that degree of love to which we are destined, we not only groan to possess God but also to possess that love which is our only happiness here below. Once Thérèse had really grasped this, the cross couldn't make her afraid any more, only God could. And then not even his majesty, but his love, his happiness, that happiness which he wants to share with us.

What is God, what is this love, what is this bliss prepared to be nailed to the cross? Why the confusion, shame and helplessness? The question is too deep for us, it is not meant for man to sound; the answer would be more than we could bear. No, my God, do not give us so much!

The quest for a moment's happiness

And yet . . . We do not stop feeling thirsty, we cannot stop hearing Christ's call, even though we are afraid; on the contrary, it becomes all the more urgent. It was only that Christ didn't want to mislead us: he couldn't reveal the essence of his joy to us before allowing us to share it, but he wanted to tell us something about it. He wanted us to know once and for all that it isn't of this world: hence he ascended the cross. And since that day, divine bliss has dwelt among us, has chosen to make its home on earth, and that home is the cross. There is no other. We keep seeking another, but never find one. We wander across the world seeking happiness, seeking a moment's happiness, but for each man there is one place, and only one, where the happiness he anxiously seeks, forever questioning landscapes, faces and hearts, is to be found; there is one moment, only one, when he will find satisfaction of all his thirst, his thirst for love, his thirst indeed for thirst. That place is the place of his cross, his own, and that moment is the hour of the cross, his hour, the one conferring meaning on all the others and which all the others have had the unique purpose of fashioning, preparing and gradually bringing to birth in him, just as all our Our Fathers, all our Hail Marys, all our De Profundises dig and inscribe daily deeper in our souls the unique Our Father, the unique Hail Mary, the unique cry of distress and love one day to explode at last from the depths of our hearts and our misery and irresistibly force the gates of heaven open.

Thus the hour of our perfect joy will also be the hour of our greatest anguish, since it is impossible on earth simultaneously to possess the appearance of happiness and its reality. Now, what we thirst for is the reality. So we thirst for the cross, which appears to be unhappiness. Bliss and the cross are so inextricably bound together for us henceforth that we cannot go on fearing the cross without fearing bliss too. We wait for it, we seek it, and when it comes we do not recognise it; or if we recognise it, we do not want it any more; it is too much for us. And we repulse it; and when we have repulsed it a hundred times, we realise that we have repulsed bliss a hundred times and that it will always be like this: that we shall always repulse it and that we shall always be athirst for it, and that we shall never escape from this thirst, and that it will hound us and torment us and obsess us and exhaust us. God's love pursues us, in pursuit of a heart open to him. Thérèse was not to escape that gravitational force dragging her towards him, since the thirst for this death had been in her, as in us, since baptism: in it we were sealed and from that day, in fact, it has been all up with us.

Perfect joy

All the same, we still have one refuge: despair, anaesthesia or revolt—and this is the worst, the cruellest of all. For at last, when we reach the shores of the promised land and have to effect our passover to God, and once we discover our creaturely and sinful condition in all its nakedness, and once we understand that divine bliss will burst the limitations of our heart and of our miserable way of being happy and of imagining what happiness and even heaven are like, how can we not recoil, not refuse?

This is why there is no other recourse but to root ourselves in the spirit of childhood. We may be indifferent to the little way of childhood; it is easy, that's the trouble. And easy too to be put off by appearances, the accidents, the Gentle Jesus style, without penetrating to the substance. But we must not forget that the Incarnation consists in God's putting himself within men's reach, of bowing when need be to their slowness and weakness, so that they will come to understand and love the essential, the uniquely necessary: God. The essential thing in the way of childhood is humble and trusting docility to the Spirit of God. He alone can make us understand and taste how sweet the Lord is, and that the consuming fire which he wishes to put in us is his very tenderness, maternal tenderness, peace beyond all understanding, sweetness so intense and so profound that it transcends all violence, not by another violence, but by its very sweetness. He alone can take us, if we wish to be 'little' enough, by what is most frail, most weak, most disabling about us, by our need to have someone who knows everything, understands everything forgives everything, repairs everything, someone who makes use of our very fear to teach us to take refuge in Love since, despite everything, beyond everything, beyond the cross, Love is still Love, happiness is still happiness and our Father is still a merciful father, terrible to the mighty but infinitely mild to the little and humble, that is, to those who trust in him and do not rely on themselves.

******

In her interminable wait for a sun that would never rise again, Thérèse defines what 'perfect joy' is. In September 1896, in the midst of the crisis from which death alone was to release her, she wrote: 'But is pure love really in my heart? Are my immense desires in fact no more than a dream, a fantasy? Oh, if so, Jesus, enlighten me . . . If my desires are rash, make them vanish, for these desires are the greatest of martyrdoms for me . . . Explain this mystery to me . . . Oh, no, the little bird won't be at all distressed . . . It will go on gazing at its Divine Sun; nothing can frighten it, neither wind nor rain, and if dark clouds come and cover the Star of Love, the little bird still won't stir; it knows that beyond the clouds the Sun is still shining, that its radiance can't be dimmed for a single second. Sometimes, true enough, the little bird's heart is battered by the storm and finds it hard to believe that anything exists apart from the encircling clouds: and for the poor weak little creature, that is the moment of *perfect joy*. What happiness for it to stay there, nothing withstanding, and gaze at the invisible light hiding from its faith!'